Men and Grief

Stories of Growth Through Struggles with Trauma and Loss

Mitch Cohen, M. ED.

Contributors: Stuart Smith, LPC, Jon Yaeger, Dom Caratzas, Robert Rainey, Derek Scott, RSW

DEDICATION

This book would not have been possible without the generosity of the contributors, which include not only the writers, but the others who we loved; who loved us; and who we lost. Those who helped all four of us get the most acknowledgment because they were the safe harbor, the guides, the unconditional loving people who held the space for us to crawl out of the deep swamp into which we were cast.

I personally have much gratitude for Stuart Smith, LPC, my grief therapist at The Link Counseling Center of Atlanta (The Link), which specializes in grief related to the loss of loved ones to suicide. I could not have made it through the first two years of grief after my wife died without Stuart. I continue to see Stuart for Supervision in my own work now as a grief counselor. The Survivors of Suicide Support Groups at The Link Counseling Center - all of us in the room having lost loved ones to suicide and listening deeply to our stories helps us recover.

Derek Scott, my Internal Family Systems (IFS) teacher and Founder of IFS Counseling Association in Canada. He is a wonderful and fully heart-based teacher, reaching students all over the world. He has contributed to so many through his work, including all of the clients of his students. His chapter on grief therapy and his therapeutic approach was such a gift to us. He never hesitated to offer his writing to us.

Jon Yaeger, my partner in crime for this project. He is one of the best writers I have ever known. He is also a friend, deeply insightful, hilarious (the fastest come-back pun lines in the history of humankind!), spiritual, kind and as compassionate as anyone I have known. His vulnerability in all things is his superpower. He also knows about fine cigars!

Robert Rainey and Dom Caratzas, the two other contributors of personal sharing, for their generous and deeply felt contributions to the book. We covered most of the bases of humanity: two white men, a black man and a brown man from Southern Europe. While the intention was to find men willing to share, these two stepped up, and thus, we had perspective from three skin tones and related experience.

Our editors, Lori Conway, Suzanne Quillian and Candice Dyer. The first piece of writing that I turned in to Lori back in 1989 was so bad, she called me into her office, because there were just way too many red markings to hand back to me for rewrite. Candice Dyer, is my friend and fellow spiritual journeyperson from Cleveland, GA. Known to frequent The Slice of Helen saloon, Candice shares her hilarious escapades and is not afraid to write about her Appalachian powerful female self and her sexuality. Suzanne Quillian performed final editing and most importantly – formatting this book for printing. It turns out this project was cathartic for her own recent grief journeys.

My friend Steve Gold, who is a fellow "Holy Rascal," and author of several books on spirituality from a Torah – Veda point of view. Steve did a final formatting and editing check and based on his experience as an author, made a number of great suggestions. He also helped with the final formatting. Steve was an inspiration and his painstaking attention to detail made this the best text possible.

My three sons: Zach, Jordan and Eric, who endured the worst hell of their lives – getting those horrible phone calls from me on the day their mother died. I still cannot imagine what it was like for them going through that shock and grief journey after that day. As they've grown, they have all become fine young men, making a difference in the world. They've also become friends more than adult children. We have group texting almost daily and share jokes, funny memes, recipes and photos of great parallel parking jobs that we accomplish. Fortunately, all have three wonderful mothers-in-law, wives, and children. Their children, my grandchildren, bring so much joy to all our lives.

My love Hannah, who has loved me, with all my stuff (neuroses and literally: bicycles, guitars, vinyl albums, books and stereo gear) for over four years. She is a wonderful psychotherapist in her own right and one of the kindest, honest, open, deep and smartest people I have ever known. My passion for learning is second to her passion. She also is a Holy Rascal, and I am blessed to have her as my life partner.

Finally, and in just the very early stages of a new grief journey, my dear dog Garcia, aged 13½, who just recently died. He was a Golden Retriever and lived up to the description of being 110% Love – for me and everyone. He was the one constant in my life through the loss of my wife, a failed relationship, three moves and had been part of our blended family for the past four years. His death was sudden and too soon, though we knew he was declining and his time in the physical world was quickly coming to an end. My heart is broken and following the lessons learned about grief, which I shared in my chapter, it will be hard, and I will get through it – in time. A long time. My friend Phil wrote about Garcia's loss, "Go home now, Garcia."

As Jon Yaeger shared with me, "we got by with a lot of support from our friends."

YOU DON'T JUST LOSE SOMEONE ONCE

You lose them over and over,
sometimes in the same day.
When the loss, momentarily forgotten,
creeps up,
and attacks you from behind.
Fresh waves of grief as the realisation hits home,
they are gone.
Again.
You don't just lose someone once,
you lose them every time you open your eyes to a new dawn,
and as you awaken,
so does your memory,
so does the jolting bolt of lightning that rips into your heart,
they are gone.
Again.
Losing someone is a journey,
not a one-off.
There is no end to the loss,
there is only a learned skill on how to stay afloat,
when it washes over.
Be kind to those who are sailing this stormy sea,
they have a journey ahead of them,
and a daily shock to the system each time they realise,
they are gone,
Again.
You don't just lose someone once,
you lose them every day,
for a lifetime.

Donna Ashworth (2021)

CONTENTS

Dedication iii

Foreword viii

1 Introduction 1

2 Dom Caratzas 6

3 Robert Rainey 21

4 Jon Yaeger 26

5 Mitch Cohen 67

6 A Therapist's Perspective 95

7 Conclusion 106

Appendix 109

References 110

Who Are You? 113

FOREWORD

Every human alive will experience loss. Loss is inevitable, from the time as a toddler that we realize our mothers are not just ours, when we have to leave the playground early, when we move away from our childhood apartment or home for the first time and when our best friend moves away from the neighborhood. Of course, loss can also be the death of a pet, friends, or loved ones. Loss is universal and unavoidable. It is never welcomed, so great is the pain it brings, along with the power to drain color and joy from our lives. However, grief is the psyche's way of processing loss, which allows us to recover and reach the point of acceptance and of life moving forward, along new paths.

Various cultures and religions give space to grief and mourning resulting from loss due to death: Jews sit Shiva for seven days after the funeral, mark the first 30 days and unveil the headstone at a cemetery after up to one year; Orthodox Christians conduct prayer vigils at defined intervals following death. Similar to Jews, Muslims have a three-day mourning period after the funeral for community visitation with mourners, and widows mourn for "four lunar months, plus 10 days." The Fore people of Papua New Guinea consumed the remains of the dead at their funerals.

The stages of grief were first proposed by Elizabeth Kubler-Ross in her 1969 book, On Death and Dying. Kubler-Ross worked with patients diagnosed with terminal illness to identify how they reacted to the initial bad news and then progressed through a process until the end of their lives (Kubler-Ross, et al., 1972). She identified five stages:

(1) Denial – Avoidance, confusion, shock
(2) Anger – Anxiety, irritation, frustration
(3) Depression – Overwhelm, helplessness, hostility, flight
(4) Bargaining – Struggling to find meaning, reaching out
(5) Acceptance – Exploring options, putting a new plan for time left

While these stages still hold true, they are not linear. Not everyone experiences all five stages (or perhaps some people repress some, such as anger). What is again important to note is that these stages are NOT linear, denial and shock are fairly typical as the first stage for everyone. The other stages are experienced as moving in and out, back and forth of the stage. In other words, a bereaved may feel anger for weeks and then it passes, only to return a few months later. In time, the bereaved passes through the difficult grief journey to a place of recovery, what some say is restoration of life, without what was lost.

This oscillation back and forth between stages of grief and recovery/restoration was studied and presented in 1999, by Margaret Stroebe and Henk Schut in their paper, "The Dual Process Model of Coping with Bereavement: Rationale and Description." In their paper, Stroebe and Schut noted that aspects of the avoidance, denial and suppression of grief were actually needed "breaks" in grief work. They are not to be avoided – as long as the process of grief work is engaged and not avoided completely, on its time and its schedule. In essence, grief comes in waves, with short breaks between the waves at first.

In the early stages of grief, the waves are huge and very close in frequency. As time passes and the oscillation between Loss-Orientation and Restoration-Orientation moves forward, the process weaves back and forth, up and down. Here is the Dual Process model for illustration:

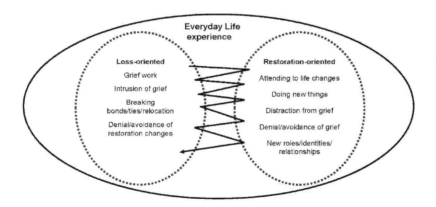

Much has been written about grief, but relatively little from the perspectives of men. Men have been socialized, particularly in Western culture to be tough. After all, many of us were taught as little boys, "big boys don't cry." This phrase was even a background line in the 1975 song by 10CC, "I'm not in love."

Frances Weller wrote in his book, The Wild Edge of Sorrow, "when grief cannot be spoken, it falls into the shadow (repressed) and re-arises in us as symptoms. So many of us are depressed, anxious and lonely. We struggle with addictions and find ourselves moving at a breathless pace, trying to keep up with the machinery of culture." (Weller, 2015)

The fact is that men feel deeply and just as deeply as women. Toughness and "strength" are not in repressing feelings; rather, real masculinity INCLUDES feeling and expressing emotions in healthy ways. Men who feel are more available to partners, friends, family and work associates. Repressed emotion in men is killing us, either through the suffering of others due to toxic masculinity, or early onset "diseases," such as uncontrolled rage, narcissistic behavior/disorders, depression, addiction, cardiovascular and even cancer.

In this book, the perspectives of four courageous and vulnerable men and two experienced, male psychotherapists have written about their experience with grief and loss. The hope is that other men will be encouraged to open up to their humanity and vulnerability and be strong by being surrendered to the pain of loss and grief. To read the sharing in this book is intended to dispense with stereotypes, and to gain new appreciation for the depth of feeling that the contributors each express.

All anyone ever wants is to share what they are experiencing, be seen, be heard and have safe space held for them. We all have wounded, young, vulnerable parts of our psyches. Through legacy burdening, shaming and role modeling, men learned to tamp down the "bad" emotions (sadness, fear, shame, hurt) and express the "good" emotions (joy and anger).

Perhaps the most unexpected revelation in the sharing of these men in this book is how genuine and profound grief can be a form of alchemy, where the heaviness of sorrow is transmuted into the pure gold of growth and genuine transformation. It may prompt not only life-changing perspectives, but also a reassessment of values and a re-ordering of priorities. And often a new sense of purpose.

At its best, grief can open the heart to newly experience and express compassion, empathy, and love, when we realize that we are never truly alone in our sadness and suffering.

Here's the irony: How can something borne of subtraction leave us such valuable gifts? We men share our stories to show you.

- Jon Yaeger and Mitch Cohen, two wounded, then healed men

1 INTRODUCTION

Mitch Cohen asked me to offer some perspectives on the theme of Men and Grief. As a therapist who regularly deals with grief, I have had countless opportunities to witness common challenges faced by men looking into the abyss generated by loss and the accompanying sense of helplessness. It is my hope that the following thoughts on mortality and vulnerability prove helpful as foundational material for the reader aiming to further an understanding of difficulties (and opportunities) faced by men dealing with loss.

Our culture may be good at many things, but grieving is usually not one of them. One may feel broken, weak, and sickened by loss. Grief is painful and messy. But grief itself is not an illness, it is rather an organic response to an emotional wounding. The challenge lies in trusting and leaning into the healing process. The confrontation with truth, pain and absence of control is often frightening and disorienting, most especially for men. Men have spent far too long trapped in their own stereotypes of how and who they are supposed to be, or perhaps equally, who they believe they cannot be. While there has been clear, though gradual improvement, there remains much to be learned. Grief is a primal, organic process, if we can allow it to be. Most often, Apollo rules and men seek refuge "upstairs" (Why waste time on feelings when there are so many thoughts to entertain?). Intellectualizing feelings is all too familiar to men. The break between head and heart can often render men awkward or speechless. In truth, a man can make himself more complete by embracing the terrifying feelings that come with loss. Loss offers an encounter with meaning, humility, humanity and with love. Stepping into loss can mean stepping into wholeness. There will be inevitable suffering, but there may also be growth. That is a choice.

Awareness of mortality can be frightening, and our individual and collective avoidance can reach enormous proportions. Ernest Becker's book "The Denial of Death" provides a brilliant and comprehensive exploration of our anxiety over mortality. (It is a great irony that Becker won the Pulitzer Prize for this book posthumously.) Mortality awakens, motivates and generates. Mortality helps inform, guide and define our humanity. When Abraham Maslow returned home after a close call with his own mortality, he reported that the view from his window had never been so beautiful — a fine example of renewed perspective and gratitude. (Becker, 2007)

The late critic Stanley Crouch shared his observations that artists from Shakespeare to Louis Armstrong benefited from including death as an essential ingredient of the humanity they explored creatively. Doing so made their work more universal, profound and honest. Conscious awareness of the transitory nature of life helps promote the cultivation of values. Experiencing loss and grieving our losses can take us deeper into our best, most meaningful selves.

At a certain level accepting mortality can be a simple process, yet profoundly liberating. As a wise retiree volunteering at funeral pyres on the Ganges very calmly stated, death need not be morose. Death, he reminded, is not the opposite of life, but merely the opposite of birth — it is all part of life! In other words, we are all, at any moment, in relationship to the endless cycle of transformation that is life. While accepting mortality doesn't exempt us from suffering a personal loss, it allows us the ability to maintain perspective in the process. Accepting mortality can make personal loss feel a little less "personal." Loss is only made much more difficult when entangled with issues of fairness or justice. Life inevitably includes loss. Fairness and justice are profoundly important human constructs, but they do not apply to our mortal nature. Nature is not fair or unfair, Nature simply is.

Grief is hard and grief is time consuming. It is not uncommon for a man seeking therapeutic support to ask right up front "how long is this going to take?" In so doing, he is of course assuming there is an established and predictable path of recovery he is embarking on; a clearly identified set of steps leading to a defined end goal. No such template exists in the journey through grief. I specifically want to emphasize the term "through". Try as we might, we cannot successfully go over, under or around the many challenges that grief brings. This is often where men find themselves trapped; in the pursuit of the avoidance referenced earlier. The journey has to be toward acceptance, and then to a healthy adaptation. "Through" does not imply an end point, but a direction. Healthy grieving requires entering the pain directly and, if possible, with humility, curiosity and trust. Psyche ("Soul") seeks healing and integration but benefits enormously from a cooperative ego. Grief is a process that occurs over time and through feelings. That process requires allowing painful experience to be accepted and integrated into our psychological reality. Time alone does far less to help than does time aided by engagement with feelings and a willingness to be in a new and undesired reality. Much of the pain in grief comes from an understandable resistance, for who wants to accept such things?

Men frequently become bound in anger. In my observations, anger in men is often a secondary emotion. Men are able to express anger exactly because it feels easier and more acceptably "masculine" than the underlying (primary) emotions of fear and hurt. Anger can be expressed without vulnerability — not so with fear and hurt. In one of the grail legends Arthur longs for a world in which "compassion is not weakness and violence is not strength." This unreconciled emotional landscape remains a dilemma in the Western male psyche. Fear and hurt deserve our respect and attention. Grieving is often about allowing rather than pursuing, but it requires courage, nonetheless. As Rollo May shared, courage does not require the absence of fear, but the will to proceed despite fear. Accepting and honoring feelings is a frightening proposition for many men. In the therapeutic process it is this very challenge that can determine the value and success of a man's journey. Jungian analyst Jim Hollis refers to the landscape of feelings as the "Swamplands of the Soul", but also the place where new life can emerge. Perhaps, as the saying goes "big boys don't cry" — but many men, those who embrace authentic experience, do cry. When they can, they do so with great and unimagined relief.

My own orientation to the therapeutic process involves some weaving of Depth Psychology, humanistic therapies, and mindfulness. All encourage encounters with the totality of human experience, and that must include mortality and loss. Far from negative, such encounters support a sense of being grounded or rooted deep in the timeless and the universal. Accepting mortality and uncertainty can be freeing. When we can accept, we tend to breathe easier. Alan Watts wrote and lectured on the wisdom of insecurity — a foreign and terrifying notion in a culture based on the illusion of control, power and ego/individualism (especially for men). One can look at accepting mortality as the rejecting of the illusion of endless power. Grief and loss can take men deep into a more mature and realistic framing of life — an emotional, psychological, philosophical and spiritual questioning and reorientation. An external, literal death (transformation) can yield a secondary transformation in the psyche of one left grieving that literal loss. One of the challenges is to recognize and differentiate a psychological or metaphorical transformation from the physical. The inability to do so can lead to hopelessness and suicidal obsessions. Acceptance of death is not about such hopelessness, but very much about a reverence and gratitude for the mystery and preciousness of life.

A man often carries repressed emotional needs precisely because he is told that he shouldn't have them. An immediate crisis is born whenever such a cruel belief is promoted. Feeling involves a vulnerable encounter with self. If vulnerability is to be avoided, then so must love and grief and growth be avoided. In other words, vulnerability, far from being the enemy, is essential to a man's healthy emotional life. Acknowledgment, acceptance, and self-compassion must replace resistance, fear and self-judgment.

Men often face challenges with an intention of "fixing" things. Some things are not to be fixed, but to be accepted, understood and integrated into a new way of being. Some mysteries are to be experienced, not solved. I consider myself fortunate to have witnessed profound growth in many grieving men. Men who may have started bewildered and doubtful but embraced the hard path of self-examination. Those who were willing to feel, to question and to confront their own true nature and accept daunting objective realities. Men who traded in fear for authenticity and were left larger and wiser for having done so. There is no pretense that such is easy, but no doubt that it can be a rewarding and transformational experience. The path of growth is a way to make meaning of loss and a way to honor those we have lost. Just as we see in the patterns of Nature, new life can indeed follow death. It will not and cannot be the same life, but a new and different life. Perhaps a life of greater awareness and increased compassion for self and others. I hope that approaching grief with more conscious awareness may help men facilitate that very process.

- Stuart Smith, LPC

2 DOM CARATZAS

A Greek Man's Story

Since I was a kid I was taught to suppress grief in all forms. Whenever something bad happened, the elders would just repeat, "Time heals everything, just be patient."

Then I started reading the journal of a friend and his sentimental confessions, and that made me understand that time does not heal everything, that you need to express what needs to be healed and share it. Hiding stuff under the rug is not helpful, especially when it comes to grief. I would like to make clear that "grief" does not necessarily mean the loss of a loved one. A lot of things cause grief, at least to me.

Those things include: a friend who doesn't want to see you anymore; an unfulfilled love; a trip you've been planning for years and has been canceled; the knowledge that someone is ill, even if you don't personally know them, but you know they're decent; of course, the loss of a loved one is on top of the list.

This is my confession and my journal. I hope it will help heal my soul or maybe inspire someone to do so.

The First Memory of Loss

I never got to meet my grandfather (from my father's side). I barely remember him, and when I went to visit my Grandma, I remember her telling me, "Go and say hi to your Grandpa." Grandpa was lying in bed, still in possession of his senses, and he would greet me with a nod and a smile. I was maybe 6 years old.

That went on for about a year. One morning I woke up and saw my father in the kitchen. He was eating grapes (that's how I can tell it was summertime). I began dragging my feet to the floor and making as many noisy movements as I could because even though he knew I was there; he didn't turn his head to look at me. I knew something was wrong. I said, "How is Grandpa today?" It was a strange question to ask in the first place because I hadn't expressed any interest in his whereabouts or well-being for weeks, maybe months. He still didn't turn to look at me and kept eating grapes from a bowl. Now that I think of it, he was probably trying to hide his tears. I repeat the question, this time in a more annoying tone: "HOW IS GRANDPA TODAY?"

He then said, "Grandpa died." I stood there as if showered with ice-cold water. He silently threw the grape sprigs in the bin, put the bowl under the sink, cleaned it, and put it in its place amongst the other dishes. I just made a U-turn, went to my room, sank under the sheets, and cried for a while.

Five minutes later I was still sad, but no longer in tears. I didn't know this man. I knew he loved me in his way, but I didn't really know him well, and he didn't know me either. I was just part of what we call "family," the kid of his son. I think my sadness had to do with interacting with other people who were really sad. I wasn't grieving. I was just sad because I could see grief around me.

The Second Loss

I could safely call us a relatively happy family back then. My brother, my father, my mother, and I were all living together in a rented flat in a good neighborhood. School was close. I had friends, and when there was no school, we would hang out in the neighborhood, playing football (soccer) in the fields and other childhood games until late at night.

Then, Mom would get out on the balcony and shout our names so we would return home for a bath and dinner. It sounds idyllic, and it was. Unfortunately, it didn't last long.

Not long after, problems started. Dad began fighting with Mom, and that included using foul language, shouting, fights, and other violence.

I became very unhappy. I remember telling one of my friends that I wanted to die, but we were just children. Two minutes after I expressed my sorrow to my friend, we played ball for a while, and then hide-and-seek and we laughed our hearts out. We were about 10 years old.

Mom's Dad moved in with us. He was a very decent man. He fought in the Greek Civil War and was sent to a remote island by the governing regime as a punishment for his beliefs. He believed in freedom of speech and the right to voice your mind. Those times were dark. Then, as things changed and he was free again, he came to stay with us.

We were young and we made his life miserable. He had several health conditions, one of them being his weakness in one foot and hand tremors. But overall, he was fairly healthy. He would give me a lot of money to go out and get him his newspaper every morning. He would say in his weird accent, "You keep the change and get yourself some condoms. Oh, wait, you're too young for that. Give me my money back!" And that made me run fast to avoid giving him his money back. He would laugh out loud every single time this happened.

We teased him at every opportunity. For example, he would ask me to turn on the water boiler so he could take a shower. I would say, "Yeah, it's on," and of course he was forced to take a shower with cold water because we intentionally turned it off.

I was part of the national U15 swimming team at age 12 or 13 and was out camping with the team and preparing for the championship. We were all sitting in the dining room and our coach was having a speech. Then the reception phone rang.

I could hear the clerk saying, "Yeah just a second. Coach: it's a phone call about one of your athletes."

I jumped up like someone had stabbed me with needles. I knew it was about me.

Coach went to the phone, and suddenly everything went dark. I remember him grabbing me by the hand and saying, "Are you all right?" Later, they told me I wasn't responding to their calls for half a minute, like I was in another dimension. Then he told me Mom was on the phone.

I went to the phone, and she coldly said, "Your Grandpa died this morning." I burst into tears. I went to my room and went under the sheets, staying there for hours. They had to force-feed me because I refused to eat. Then I threw up. The coach called home and said they should come pick me up because I no longer had a reason to be there with the rest of the team.

On our drive home, I remember them asking me if I wanted to attend the funeral. I said, "No, I do not." Those were words that just spontaneously came out of my mouth. It was my first reaction to something that I knew would be very painful, and I wanted to avoid pain.

Jerry

I remember the night when Dad came to our room and told me, "Come with me, I want to show you something. Get dressed."

I knew that when things like that happened, it was the moment of our day, or even the week or month. It had to be something extraordinary, something explicit to draw our attention like that, and to have us get dressed in the middle of the night to go outside – somewhere. It had to be huge.

I heard the little puppy cries. It was Jerry, a German Shepherd, just a few days old. He was crying, likely asking for his mother. I hugged him in tears, and he licked me. I said to Dad, "I love him." Dad cried too. He said, "All yours, but take good care of him, all right?" I answered, "I swear."

Unfortunately, Mom didn't like Jerry. She was too busy to take care of him; Dad was always at work, and we were too young to take him for a walk, etc., which caused problems. She recently confessed that she put him in the car, drove far away from home, and abandoned him. Then she felt guilty and returned. He was just sitting there, in the middle of nowhere waiting to be picked up by someone. She told me this now. Had she even mentioned it at that time, it wouldn't have ended well.

Jerry died at the age of four after getting hit by a car. Dad found him several days later. We all cried for this dog. He was my friend. My companion. I would talk to him about my thoughts, my problems, my concerns and he would stand there, listen to me, maybe not understand the exact words, but he would get my feelings exactly. He would wag his tail to comfort me and nod his head against my chin to make me composed.

I still haven't gotten over this loss. There are tears as I write these words. The truth is, you never get over a loss of a loved one.

I think Jerry made me understand what dogs are about and what kind of unconditional love you get without them demanding anything back — just a hug and a pet on the back. Since then, I've had at least one dog by my side: a stray or an abandoned one, or a shelter dog, or a rescue dog. There always will be at least one. I've made sacrifices to have them, and I do not regret a single minute or a single cent spent for their well-being. Jerry taught me this. Not a teacher. Not a person. Not school. A dog. Not "a" dog. Jerry.

Divorce

In the beginning of 1988, all of sudden, things started taking the wrong turn. Dad asked me to start sleeping in their bedroom with Mom because he wanted to sleep on my bed. I objected. I told him, "my bedroom, my bed, my rules." It wasn't an attempt to make things straight with them again because I understood things weren't going well — I wasn't making such complex thoughts at the time. I just didn't want to part with my bed or my childhood, and I didn't want to violently enter the adults' world. That's how I was seeing it. Of course, I caved.

The first few nights in the master bedroom were weird. I was 13, at the beginning of my sexual maturity. I was having wet dreams and being on the same bed with Mom didn't help. She wasn't someone I could talk to about these things. I started feeling embarrassed about my sexual urges and had to find excuses to spend a lot of time in the toilet. At the same time, Dad was starting to become distant, being dragged down to the path of depression and unhappiness.

It was late September and Mom asked me if I wanted to join her for a walk. At first I declined, trying to finish up a stage in "Shinobi," but she insisted I go with her, and even bribed me with all sorts of treats, from ice cream to marshmallow and from cheesecake to chocolate. Who would say no? We walked for about 20 minutes, when I saw Dad's car parked in an alley. I said, "Whew, is Dad coming with us too? Great!" She asked why am I saying this and where did this come from? With all of my innocence, I pointed my finger and I said, "But Dad is here, there's his car."

It turned out Dad was having an affair. He left home three days before Christmas, 1988. The way they presented it to us, well, I wouldn't nominate them as candidates for parents of the year. It was a cold, dark, afternoon. I was playing a game on my computer; Dad was on the phone, and I could hear him say, "No, I will stay at my mother's tonight, so call me there to arrange to get you the money in the next few days." I was sad, knowing what was going on. Dad came to my room, kissed me on the cheek and said, "bye now," and then he burst into tears. I stood there frozen, while he closed the door behind him. I cried so hard then; I shall never forget it. Now that I think of it, I think those were tears of grief and relief at the same time. I knew I was going to miss him, but I wasn't going to miss all the anger and fights and door slams and shouting and ugly words, and those that were haunting me for years and became a daily thing.

The same day, Mom gathered me and my brother in the kitchen, sat us at the kitchen table and said (and I remember her exact words 33 years later): "Your father has left us. He abandoned us. He abandoned you. He is having another woman, and he decided to abandon all of us to our fate. You need to decide now if you want to stay and live with me here in this house or you want to follow him and live with him and that other woman."

Of course this blackened my soul and caused a mixture of feelings including anger and hatred, especially against my own father for his betrayal. That lasted until New Year's Eve, when he showed up under our house and started honking his horn and making signals for us to go down and get in the car with him. I remember us sitting by the window and looking at him and Mom yelling, "Don't you dare go down. Don't you dare!"

At that age I started to become very disobedient, but it felt "right." I opened the door, and made a few hesitant steps toward the stairwell, but then I turned 90 degrees and jumped down and burst through the door. I got in the car. Dad looked at me and said, "How y' holding up, pal?" I awkwardly replied, "OK," and then he cuddled me. I cried. I told him I hate him for leaving us. He cried. He said he had to go because he was very unhappy and couldn't stand it any longer. He said that this doesn't mean he did not love me and promised to be there for me no matter what. He added that this doesn't mean we shouldn't see each other, that we can build a new relationship, stronger and more honest. I remember every single word he said. We cried a lot. I am crying now while I'm typing these words and can barely see the screen. He reached out and gave me some pocket money. I opened the door and left. I wasn't happy, but I was relieved. Suddenly I realized my father wasn't a bad man – he didn't abandon us; he didn't abandon me; he was just unhappy with his life and wanted to change it. I went home.

Mom said, in these exact words, "You should be ashamed, running to him, he abandoned you and you went inside his car and took his money as if you're some kind of beggar." Being in a bad way, I mumbled, "Oh, fuck off," and went to my room. Luckily, I don't think she ever heard it. My brother was very upset and didn't go down to meet him. Eventually Dad left after waiting for him for a few hours.

They filed for a divorce shortly thereafter. It turned out Dad was horrible at keeping his finances straight, and he couldn't afford to support himself, let alone to pay child support as the court demanded. It also turned out that he took a bank loan after he faked my Mom's signature as a credit voucher. I overheard Mom talking on the phone with her sister and saying, "Yes, I can put him behind bars, but I don't want to do this to him, we've spent a lot of years together, he's the father of my children, I don't want to punish him like that. Yeah he's a scum but he doesn't deserve to be put in jail." I still appreciate this, after all these years.

Grandma Elisabeth

Dad's mother, Grandma Elisabeth, loved me very much. I could sense her face expression change every time I called her and said, "Hey Grandma." Each and every time I called her, she invited me to go pay her a visit and that always included a great meal, chocolate, and big pocket money for me. Sometimes, I would even ring her bell uninvited. I'm not ashamed to admit that sometimes I would just go there to get my pocket money and feel comfortable buying my girlfriend a ticket to the movies or schnapps. I remember once I went there without notice and rang her front door. She opened up but forgot to wear her denture. I was shocked; I couldn't stop staring at her mouth, until she realized something was wrong, so she went to the bathroom for 20 seconds then came back and gave me her best smile. And cash. And a chocolate bar.

When I rang her and told her I was coming, she would go to have her hair done, wear her nicest clothes and sit there and expect me. After I ate her always exceptional meal, I would lie on the sofa and fall asleep, and she would come with a blanket and cover me – even if it was the middle of the summer. I objected once and she said with that funny accent, "Ayew, weather's funny, you can'a catch ay cold, you're a youngster ain't ya," but in funny slang.

Grandma suddenly got sick and was hospitalized for a long time. Doctors said it was cancer. She was 85. She died peacefully one morning.

I mourned. I decided I wanted to grieve in isolation. I went to a remote beach and sat there for hours. I then took a bus, but intentionally chose the wrong way so I could spend as much time sitting by the bus window watching the scenery. Eventually I went home. I was 23 and a student in the university at that time. It was my first grieving as an adult. I could feel it in the pores of my skin.

I remember I would detour and go by Grandma's tomb every two days, or something like that. I wasn't crying – not every time, at least. I would simply go there and take care of the tomb; clean it, add fresh flowers and just leave. It was perhaps a five-minute visit, but it felt good. It felt like I had to mourn a little longer. Or maybe pay my respects a little longer.

Until one day.

When the bus stopped, I got down and walked the path as usual, but the tomb wasn't there. Dad had not paid for a renewal, so they had her removed. I screamed inside. I called him, and he said he didn't have money to pay their outrageous renewal fees, so they just dug out the grave and had someone else buried there. When my anger eased, he told me the amount they were asking, and it was insane. He told me, "It doesn't matter if there is a tomb with her name or not. As long as you memorize and mention her, she will never die." He was right.

Betrayal

Some time after Grandma's death, we were notified that her will was going to be opened and read. We were told that the house where she had lived — a three-bedroom apartment downtown, the flat that was always my sanctuary, where I always found a place to eat, sleep and be cuddled — was left to me and my brother, 50 percent each. That was her last will.

Dad was happy.

Mom was happy. For different reasons.

I was excited.

I was 23, and now I could go to the university and then walk back home and have a place of my own. That's it: A new era just began. Thanks, Grandma! I hadn't felt so happy in my life.

After I graduated from college, I was called to serve obligatory army duty, so I left to do that. I was 300 miles away from home, but at least I was independent and alone, far away from everything that would darken my mind and my soul.

My cousin, who is a lawyer, called and asked when I would get my next week off, and when I would be back in my hometown. I was surprised by the phone call: even though we always had a very fond relationship, it was puzzling me. "In two weeks, but why do you ask?" I replied. And without a second's hesitation she said, "What do you mean? To sign the contracts. Didn't your Mom tell you?"

As it turned out, Mom decided to sell the house – the house that belonged to me (half of it anyway). I objected to my cousin, and started yelling that I'm not selling anything, I don't care what she's told you, this house stays, and I don't give a fuck. She then said "Listen, don't put me in the middle of this, talk to your mother. The buyer has already taken a bank loan to pay for this house and they can sue you if the deal breaks." I was devastated.

I called Mom and said words to her that no child should say. At that time, it felt right. I was very, very angry. I felt betrayed again, left out from such an important decision, which I'm just learning of from my cousin? To be invited to sign the contracts? She didn't have the slightest courtesy to talk to me about such a serious matter? I felt that I had the right to speak to her like that.

I called Dad and told him what was going on. He burst into tears. It was the house he grew up in. We agreed to have a meeting in two weeks when I got back, to see if anything could be done. Unfortunately, nothing could be done, and I signed the contracts.

That day was the day that the glass had broken between me and Mom, and I hated her for several reasons: for undermining me; for taking a revenge-decision to sell the house of the mother of the man who betrayed her; and for not discussing it with me.

Many years later, I discovered that the reason behind her wanting to sell the house so much was because Dad had put her in trouble with another bank loan that was due, and she was facing jail time. Shit was getting real. She had to find a lot of money fast to pay bail. I did not know that until recently.

Scavenger of Human Sorrow

As time went by, my relationship with Dad got stronger. We would meet downtown every other day, have dinner, and talk about girls. I met his new wife. He didn't invite me to their wedding; I found out they got married when I saw pictures of their wedding hanging on their walls. She was nice enough, but I never made peace with the thought that she was trying to replace Mom. Even though I hated Mom at that time, she was Mom. The new wife helped him escape from debt up to a point. She was kind with me and she seemed to love him very much – and that was enough for me.

Our relationship got even stronger as time went by. I would call him and take him to lunch and speak to him about this new girl. Then, about a car I wanted to buy. Later, about a good job I found which would give me enough to move out of Mom's house and have a place of my own. He gave me some money. I knew he didn't have any, so I gave it back. He insisted and said that's what he can give me now to start a new life. It wasn't much but it was from his heart. I took it. I thanked him for it and bought us dinner.

Many years later, I was invited by his wife to their beach house for a glass of wine. When I got there, he was drunk. That was extremely rare – he didn't drink. He would drink socially, but I had never seen him drunk before. He was in a very good mood. He fell asleep eventually and his wife had a talk with me. She was concerned.

He was careless and didn't take care of himself at all. She told me he had skin lesions all over and begged him to go to a doctor for a check-up, but he would not want to hear about it. She asked me to look through his shirt now that he was asleep and see for myself. I did. It looked awful. She asked me to help to convince him.

I called him the next day. I told him that I've made an appointment with a dermatologist, and we should be there at 5 p.m. He said OK.

He never showed up. I called him, and he told me, "Get yourself examined and see if everything is all right with you and then I'll show up." I was furious. He hung up.

The following day I went to see him, and he was drunk again, sleeping. I woke him up and told him that he most likely has skin

16

cancer, and that he'll die. I told him, "It's not time yet to leave me alone and unprotected in this world, you're all I've got," and asked him to promise me he'll take care of it. Deaf ears.

I remember I went to my car, started the engine and was so emotionally overwhelmed that I burst into tears and couldn't stop crying for some 20 minutes. Then I started driving home and had to stop again and cry. I knew this would not end well.

Turns out, the lesions went away, and he was fine for a couple of years. My urges to consult a doctor fell to the floor, ignored once again. That was until March 16, 2013.

The Disease

On March 16, 2013, I got a call from Dad's wife who said I should pay them a visit as soon as possible. She sounded very worried, but she is a high-strung person who gets upset about everything. A small corner in my mind said that it would be nothing serious. I did not pay them a visit the same day because I had already planned to go out with friends and have a few beers.

She called me the next day, very upset, and started yelling at me and asking why didn't I come to see my father. I was puzzled and – long story short – I went by their house.

She asked me to go somewhere to talk privately. Dad became upset and started swearing. I knew something was very, very wrong. She told me that Dad has lost mobility; he would walk slowly and frequently fell. Because he was 6 feet tall and more than 240 pounds, it was not easy for him to stand up on his own after he fell, so they called in neighbors to help him get up.

I was shocked. I asked him to stand up and come toward me, and he objected. I got angry and asked him to do as he was told, for once in his life. He did. I could tell that his movements were abrupt; his pace was slow, and his steps were very small.

The following day I took him to a neurologist. He didn't want to come. I forced him into the car. He had lost a lot of his strength and couldn't resist. Three years earlier I wouldn't have tried to force anything upon him, as I would be dead meat.

Parkinson's.

The doctor said it will get worse, and prescribed drugs to slow down the disease, and sent us home. I was devastated.

His wife was taking good care of him – I'll give her that. She had an eye disease that progressed too, and nowadays she's almost blind. Back then, she could barely see, which complicated their everyday life even more.

I hired a woman who would help them with everyday tasks such as laundry and cooking and had someone on standby for house tasks like carrying heavy items, maintaining the garden, fixing a broken window, and things like that.

The disease progressed rapidly. Soon I received a call that he had been admitted to the hospital after passing out. I rushed to the hospital, and they explained that he suffered a bowel rupture due to Parkinson's meds causing constipation. He lost a lot of blood, requiring immediate surgery.

Dad survived the surgery, but the next day he went into a coma due to pneumonia. Pneumonia was caused by the laxatives used for bowel prep for surgery, which were absorbed by his kidneys, further complicated by the Parkinson's. They told us, judging by his history, that his chances of surviving the ICU were about five percent. But it's better than nothing; he would die anyway. Those were the doctor's words, exactly.

I remember myself slowly walking through the hospital corridors and punching my fists against the walls. I even broke the carpal bone on my right fist.

After he was in a coma for three days, I went to pay him a visit. When I opened the ICU door, there he was, with his eyes open. I screamed. He couldn't move, so he just rolled his eyes towards me. "Is he awake? Why didn't you tell me?" There was a nurse in the room, she said he woke up a few hours ago. He wouldn't talk, but he could communicate. I kissed him and told him I would go to call everyone and tell them the good news and everything will be fine. His eyes watered. I will never forget that day. I will never, ever forget the sight of his blue eyes wide open. Not ever.

The next day he was discharged from the ICU. Doctors said he's a fighter. They took him back to the regular clinic and then they asked me to follow them for consultation. He needed to be admitted to a rehabilitation center to help him start moving his legs again and help him get better.

Dad stayed there for about two months. Eventually he started talking and kept complaining that he wanted to go home. He steadily improved. A few days before he was due to be discharged, he spiked a fever.

March 31, 2016 was the last time I saw him. When I went to visit, there was no one else in the room, and I closed the door. I looked at him. He looked terrible. The only thing that remained of the once strong, vivid man was his eyes. He looked at me. I kissed him on his forehead. I knew the end was coming. I told him, "I'm so happy I had you in my life. Thank you." He cried. I cried. I couldn't stand it. I turned my back, opened the door and left.

He died on the dawn of April 2, 2016. The nurse who was on watch said she checked on him at 3:30 in the morning and he was calm and peaceful. That calmed me. At least he wasn't in pain. The last one of us who saw him alive was my brother, who paid him a visit – after not giving a damn if his father was still alive or not for more than 2 years – one day before he died.

I'm pretty sure he was so stubborn that had waited for his other son to pay him a visit before passing away.

The Next Day

I took care of the funeral. I was in shock. I thought I'm going to have a heart attack, but I didn't. I knew he'd want me to keep going.

I asked my wife to leave me alone for a couple of days. She moved into her parents' house. I shut the blinds, closed the curtains, deactivated my phone, sat on the sofa, and drank.

I drank an impossible quantity of strong liquor and beer. I'd fall asleep on the sofa, wake up; go to the toilet; throw up, then drink again until wasted.

That lasted for three days. I believe the books describe this phase as the peak of the mourning period.

It's been five years and I haven't gotten over the death of my beloved father. I still get depressed when I think about it. Sometimes I remember the good times we had together, sometimes the bad ones. I try to not remember or over-think the last few years where he was sick because these were extremely hard times and I like to forget about them.

I think that writing these thoughts helps me toward that goal.

I've made peace with Mom and my brother, too. I find it hard to forgive everything they've done, but after giving it some thought I've decided to give them another chance.

I started paying her visits, sometimes staying for lunch. Our phone calls became more normal in tone and frequency. The birth of our baby boy three months ago gave her another boost in life on this planet. She's so happy and excited, she calls me now every day. Surprisingly I pick up and tell her all the news.

I also made a fresh start with my brother. We even went out for a beer.

Hoorah!

Conclusion

Writing these words was soothing for my soul. I've cried – a lot – while bringing back all those memories, and now I feel relieved.

3 ROBERT RAINEY

A Black Man's Story

In early March of 2013, I received a call from my son Robert's aunt that he had passed away.

He had been living in Reno, Nevada. Like most parents, this was unbelievable news. We had lost his twin brother Richard in May of 1996. Surely God wasn't letting this happen again. Needless to say, I sobbed for hours. And it appeared that I was all alone. I was living in the inner city of Detroit, Michigan. If I'm being honest, I was very unhappy with my life at the time. So, this news just seemed to pile on to that unhappiness.

A myriad of thoughts were racing through my mind. What happened exactly? How could I have prevented his death? Was I a good father, etc. Why did God allow this to happen again? Yes, that question persisted, though I knew it wasn't a fair question. But in my moment of despair and anger, I needed someone to blame. And I went straight to the creator.

Just to shed some light on my blaming God, back in 1996 when Richard made his transition, I was devastated! I received the news via voicemail. It felt like a part of me had been ripped away. I seemed to be throwing up until I had nothing left. It felt like someone had reached inside of me and pulled my guts out.

Within days I was in Florida where his mother and her family lived. Although, we didn't have the best relationship, in that moment we had something in common — the loss of our son.

I remember vividly that I didn't want to ask God the big question. Why? I had been growing religiously. I was attending First Baptist Atlanta at the time. My heart was telling me not to question Ricky's passing and that there's a reason for everything, sometimes beyond our understanding.

Even though I was living in Atlanta and my children lived in south Florida with their Mom, I felt we had a special bond. So here I am in early 2013 experiencing the same dream; at least I wished it were a dream! But as each day passed by, traveling to Florida, the funeral, etc. I realized it wasn't a dream.

Overcoming Grief

I mentioned earlier that I had been growing religiously, but I left out a few things that helped me. Yes, my growing relationship with God played a key role in overcoming my grief — the way he gave me peace during my trip to Florida. My friends and family reached out seemingly just at the right times. But I was putting on a very brave face while breaking down on the inside.

Soon, as if God-sent, an old colleague, Mitch Cohen, who had been checking in on me, suggested that I talk to a therapist. I took his suggestion under advisement, but in my head my ego was telling me that I didn't need that. I mean come on; I was a former Marine! Marines simply deal with it. Fortunately, a couple of weeks later I called my friend and asked for the number to the therapist because I was losing myself. I was having some serious headaches. My blood pressure was through the roof. Those were some of the symptoms of keeping things bottled up on the inside.

Seeing a therapist was the best thing that happened to me at the time. I called and set up an appointment within the next week. What a blessing. This former Marine had been brought to his knees. In other words, I was broken. The loss of my son had brought to the forefront issues from the past that I had suppressed which I was able to get out with this wonderful therapist. Eventually there were lots of tears and healing simply through getting things that had been kept in the dark out in the light. The light is an incredible antidote to the dark. The light is a cure for internal pain.

Flash back to Robert's passing in 2013 and the "here we go again feeling." It was unbelievable, yet I seemed to be in a better place in terms of coping. Oh, don't misunderstand me. The pain of losing yet another child was very hurtful and bitter. But something was different, and I knew that God was guiding me through my grieving period.

Over the years I had moved away from traditional religion and started studying spirituality. Why is this important? Because spirituality seemed to be more about love as opposed to fear. Something never felt right about God being associated with fear. I needed to know that my boys and my mother who had made her transition in September of 2010, were being loved. Divinely loved.

In November of 2012, I had attended a coaching seminar in New York City, given by Dr. Robert Holden. To this day I believe that I was divinely guided there. At the time Life Coaching was becoming very popular and I knew that field wanted to help people be their best selves. I was supposed to attend a coaching program earlier that year with a friend, but the timing wasn't good for me. So, I decided to wait until later in the year.

I knew the names of a few nationally as well as internationally known coaches who had certification programs, but I had come across Robert's information as if I were directed to it. It was as if his name had leaped off the page at me. In hindsight, there was an energy that seemed to be emanating as I read his page. Although I went away from his website on several occasions I knew when I first saw his ad that I would be attending his workshop.

Now, what does all of this have to do with overcoming grief? It was the beginning of a lot of things. My understanding of our purpose in life while here on this earth. My understanding that we are not simply these human bodies. My understanding of death and most importantly my understanding of God's Divine love for us.

Again, what does all of that have to do with overcoming grief? Well, I noticed the more I embraced God's love (God as love) and us as his creation, I realized we are an extension of that. Understanding that as spirits having a human experience, we're given opportunities to be our best selves. To be love. Divine love! To be an extension of that which gives us life. And that in this world of duality and delusion there will be things happening good and bad.

There are tragedies every moment of every day, be it the winds of Mother Nature or our own self-inflicted mortal wounds. And, of course, oftentimes these bodies become ravaged with disease. I learned that loved ones and friends will at some point be transitioning into another life.

The key is to understand our role as spirits because let's face it, "we" will be leaving at some point, too. We must find our center with God. We must love each other as brothers and sisters. Be it family members, neighbors, strangers, or even our enemies.

My healing was happening in real time the more that I embraced this love. Agape love. One might define it as unconditional love. I was starting to find peace in life again.

The more I embraced Divine love, the greater was my ability to be grateful for the time that I had shared with my sons. Why is this important? I know people who still suffer today after 10 to 15 years of losing loved ones because they have not let them go. But when you thank God for the time we were able to share with those who have made their transition, there is a type of freeing. We must let them go without attachment.

Around two months after Robert made his transition, I was home and all of a sudden, I heard a voice say to me: "I'm all right Dad, I'm all right Dad." It was Robert's voice. It was as if it were coming from a never-ending tunnel. It wasn't loud or overbearing. It was good to hear his voice, but it was better knowing that he was all right.

I share this with you because as I stated earlier, we're all going to make our transition at some point. And we must learn two things that have helped me overcome grief. One, death is not real. Again, we are spirits having a human experience. We simply leave these bodies. And two, we must learn to surrender. The only thing we have control over in this life is how we respond to things in this world of duality and delusion. Will we exchange love and gratitude for anger and blame? I choose love and gratitude!

In good times or bad, build up your prayer chest. Too often we wait until we're in a really bad place or until tragedy strikes to spend time in prayer and meditation. Prayer and meditation give us inner strength in those bad times which will surely continue to show up although they may look different for each of us.

Find moments daily, morning and night, to spend time in prayer and meditation even if it is just five minutes. Our prayers are not only helpful in our own trials but in the lives of others as well. Remember we're all connected to the One Divine Spirit.

I write this with much love and respect for those who continue to struggle with the grief and loss of their loved ones and friends.

4 JON YAEGER

A White Man's Story

Introduction

Phil Foster, a mutual friend, introduced me to Mitch Cohen. Cohen leads an ecumenical book club with members from diverse faiths and professions, and I joined his group.

Cohen studied to become an engineer; a Rabbi; and a counselor. However, nothing prepared him for his wife's suicide several years ago.

With some awareness of my own losses, Mitch invited me to collaborate with him and others on a work about men, and our perceptions and reactions to grief.

Apparently there is much written (and studied) about grief in general, but not a lot about how men in particular react to and grapple with it (culturally, we men tend to ignore, repress, and guard strong against expressing grief, lest it appear as a character flaw or weakness). And so we silently "soldier on," bearing our wounds and losses and scars, which rarely heal on their own.

I recognized the catharsis of writing about painful personal experience. The possibility that it might be familiar and perhaps helpful to some others was added impetus to agree to participate.

I know that I can't speak for all or even other men about the topic of grief, but I can share what I have experienced and come to know about it – a singular voice among many.

My account follows a rough chronological order, but it's not simply a catalog or compendium. It has been a journey – and in retrospect, an invaluable one.

A Journey Unfolding

"I am a man of constant sorrow
I've seen trouble all my day…"
– Traditional American Folk Song

Loss is universal, and so are the accompanying feelings of sadness and grief. Sorrows multiply with age, as we lose our parents; our friends; and eventually we go too.

My grief started as a child, even before I knew what grieving was. It returned throughout my life with notable frequency and intensity, mostly without warning.

Somehow – over time – trauma and sorrow became catalysts for personal growth and transformation. This thief of happiness managed to leave something precious behind: a little wisdom and a lot of gratitude.

My healing did not occur in solitude. The love and support I received from family, friends, clergy and professionals during the difficult times and in quieter interludes were essential to the process.

This is my story.

The Sponge Effect

Although I was excited by it, Christmas was never a truly happy time for me as a child. My neurotic and perennially unhappy relatives would gather and stay in our home. Ancient sisters would fight; doors would slam; and tears and recriminations would flow. Not understanding any of it, I nonetheless absorbed it like a sponge. They loaned me their grief and sorrow, and I managed to invest it.

Like a canary in a coalmine, I sensed the toxicity of our family get-togethers before it manifested in overt behavior. Any extended family gathering filled me with the fear of impending sadness: sadness over love lost; opportunities squandered; and unhappy, dysfunctional marriages. All in a language I couldn't understand or process, yet conveying emotions I couldn't avoid.

On another occasion, I vividly recall a trauma at my grandfather's dark and foreboding house in Riverdale. I was three or four, with relatives gathered in the backyard. I was stripped naked in front of everyone and told to swim in a small, poured concrete "pool." I felt emotionally and physically exposed: vulnerable and miserable.

Summer in Niantic, CT ca. 1960

For what it is worth, years later a psychic suggested that I was an unusually sensitive and empathic child, and that I was regularly overwhelmed. She added that when I was about five, I had figured out how to turn it off enough to cope.

My sensitivity may be muted, but it is not gone. Sometimes I still manage to tune into people and sense – if not adopt – their feelings. I may intuit feelings and images while in their company, sometimes in specific detail. It is unsettling if I ask about it and there is confirmation.

Reflection: One doesn't have to "own" or be fully aware of grief to feel its effects. Proximity to grief and sadness may suffice. I could not articulate my feelings, but I was no less sensitive to them, and those of others.

My distress fell under the family's emotional radar, so I received no acknowledgment or special handling.

Do sensitive people feel grief more acutely, more frequently, or longer? Maybe there is a "spectrum" of sorrow that encompasses the range of human experience; and perhaps genes and personalities factor into where we land on it.

Doggone It

I was about seven or eight when Dad decided it would be a good idea to get a family dog. In some ways, it was really his dog. He probably softened up Mom with the promise that I would learn about caring and responsibility by having a pet, although she knew who would be taking care of it once the novelty faded.

I vaguely recall going to pick from a litter of Labrador Retrievers, but the smell of the new pups was unforgettable. I named the dog Licorice, and it stuck. Nobody else liked the name.

I remember housebreaking and early training. The dog grew rapidly. He needed no tutorial to fetch (as his breed implies), and he often retrieved presents of dead birds and other creatures.

Licorice was a great companion, but a problem arose: I developed an allergy, and breathing became difficult. My parents sent me to an allergist to confirm the cause, or maybe to deliver the bad news – there was no way to manage the allergy, and so the dog would have to go.

**Tempting Licorice with a bone on the front porch
at 611 Euclid Ave in Elmira, NY**

Upon hearing the bad news, I told the hapless physician how I truly felt: "I hate you!", trying to ruin his day, too.

Dad promised that Licorice was going to a man in the country, where he could live happily on a farm. That was likely a euphemism for having an animal euthanized, but I'll never know.

Nonetheless, the dog's departure was my first major loss.

Among my favorite movies is Lasse Hallström's poignant and sad film, "My Life as a Dog." The movie was based upon a semi-autobiographical book, and it has plenty of parallels to my own childhood.

In one scene, his distant uncle promises to take care of Ingemar's beloved dog in his absence. The young boy is devastated when another character later tells him that the dog was destroyed.

Ingemar was self-reflective:

"People shouldn't think so much. 'Time heals all wounds,' Mrs. Arvidsson says. Mrs. Arvidsson says some wise things. You have to try to forget." (Hallström, 1985)

I waited 50 years to get another dog.

The Twins

It's February 1965. My pregnant mother went into the hospital with labor pains, her belly as fat as a spider's. Knowing that her husband was terminally ill, her doctors spared her the shock that she was carrying two until they both emerged into the world. Surprise!

Suzanne arrived first; Lisa emerged four minutes later.

I was elated when I heard the news. I ran around the neighborhood, summoning friends and neighbors with my fingers in a V, shouting, two! TWO!

Tiny at birth, the twins were incubated under lights at Elmira's Arnot Ogden Hospital until they were matured sufficiently to come home. They slept in matching bassinets and there were two of everything.

My sister Robin and I would take turns putting the infants in our own beds, feeling their warm little bodies and smelling their sweetness and innocence. Nothing quite compares to that intoxicating odor of goodness and promise.

The twins were the bright lights in our lives. There is no better way to avoid sadness than to focus upon the ones you love.

Suzy & Lisa in the little red wagon. Ca. 1968

Their personalities changed as they grew older, and sometimes they swapped roles. Suzy was dominant until Lisa eventually found her groove, and thereafter Lisa was usually the impetus for their passions and projects.

Preemptive Grief

My father was diagnosed with spinal cancer in his late 30s. He lived for about a year more, and died a month shy of his 40th birthday. I was eight at the time of diagnosis; and nine when he died.

In those days (the 1960s), a cancer diagnosis was feared and usually hushed, as if it were shameful – or contagious. There was no chemotherapy or effective treatment for sarcoma beyond surgical excision.

The reticence about discussing terminal disease reflected the reluctance of the times to confront the reality and inevitability of death. Children were "spared" at the expense of grief and closure. Fortunately, our awareness and understanding of how children process and react to loss has improved since then.

I knew Dad was sick, but in my experience with chickenpox and colds, sick people got well – and so I assumed Dad would, too.

David Yaeger was a street-wise sailor and engineer from Brooklyn who was "raised by wolves" in a very dysfunctional family. He was of the WWII generation that did not express feelings, yet he was well liked and respected in our town. The love he dispensed was tough love, typical of his generation.

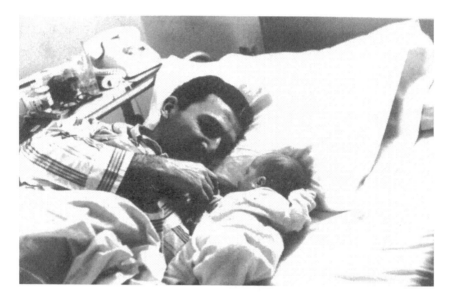

Dad visiting with one of the twins, 1965

Dad could be tender, but he was also someone to be feared, given the corporal punishment that I received fairly often. I do have happy memories of him teaching me to ride a bike and to fish, or visiting the glass manufacturing plant where he worked. He made me proud. I adored him and wanted more.

Unfortunately, those happier times were eclipsed by the last year of his life as his health deteriorated, and the norms and safety rails of my family dissolved. I realize now that I was depressed and grieving for things that went missing from my childhood.

As Dad became more immobile, a hospital bed was set up in my bedroom, now converted into a sick bay. I was dispossessed and relegated to an upstairs "sleeping porch." It had dark walnut paneling in the style of the 60s. The baseboard heating provided a meager defense against the long, cold winters.

The house was a flurry of activity. The infant twins needed constant tending, as did my father. Friends and medical staff were Dad's frequent visitors, but I was not.

Children were second-class citizens in those days; my maternal grandmother often reminded us that, "children are to be seen, and not heard." That did not stop me from being a needy kid, always vying for attention. I can only imagine Dad's terror in knowing that he would leave behind a young wife and four children before his 40th birthday. He was likely at a loss for words to say to me. My visits were intermittent and often cut short by my father or his caretakers.

One of the attendants was a male nurse, who was gay and rumored to have been a pedophile. According to Mom, he was hired to do unpleasant things, and he had an essential role. She was vigilant to minimize our contact, and so I saw Dad even less.

It took a toll. I suffered at school. I wanted attention yet could not pay it. My report cards noted that I had difficulty focusing. I was sent away to summer camp for a month to get me out of the house and from under foot. Few kids my age stayed that long, and it seemed interminable. I made no attempt to hide my sadness; I just wanted to go home.

Kids can sense vulnerability, and I was bullied by an older camper named "Greenie." One day the bullying abruptly stopped, and he became friendly and solicitous. There must have been an intervention.

Dad's doctor gave him LSD to try to help to manage his depression. It was a novel drug; the treatments were experimental. Instead of it helping, my father had a hellishly bad trip, imagining that he was floating down the Styx – the river of death. Mom said it broke his spirit. He wrote it all down, and Mom kept his journal for a time, but I never saw it. At some point he attempted suicide by saving and swallowing barbiturates. He went into a coma and recovered.

My father was my grandfather's only son. Louis Yaeger was a very wealthy stockbroker and investor who came to visit his sick son only once. Making money was more important. While he was on his deathbed, Dad pleaded with his father to take care of the family financially, but Louis flatly refused. No one knew why. Yet he paid for Robin's and my education at boarding schools and colleges.

I mention these horrors because they poisoned the well at 611 Euclid Avenue even more. It would be difficult for any parent to reveal and discuss disease and impending death or sexual predation with a child. I sensed the household stress, but I did not know why, which made me feel more disconnected and isolated.

During the interval from diagnosis to death, joy and normality were sucked from my childhood, a silent process without words or comprehension. I was not aware of what was missing, but my sense of loss and grief was real, and it preceded death itself.

Reflection: Death and grief go together. But grief may come with any perceived loss – a job; a lover; a missed opportunity; declining health or fortunes; and abandonment. I lost the usual safety and security of childhood, and things I took for granted. The instability of my family and the sadness I experienced before my father's death multiplied my distress afterwards. If I felt ignored before, I felt abandoned now, left behind by Mom's need to tend to her husband and her babies.

A Devastating Surprise

During the year of my father's illness, I was shuttled around to friends and neighbors' homes in Elmira for sleepovers. I was at the Olmsteads when Mom went into labor with the twins. So I didn't think much about it when my sister Robin and I were invited to the Stein's, less than a block away for a "sleepover."

Nana, my maternal grandmother, came over in the morning to tell us that Dad had died. She was composed and matter of fact about it. Maybe she did her crying before she reached us, or it was just the familiar pattern of men in her life dying too early.

It was as though I was at the beach scanning the shore, only to turn around to face a tsunami. Great waves of grief washed over me, and I was at its mercy: powerless to hide or flee.

Dad was gone without warning. I never had the chance to say goodbye. There was no closure or blessing. I was devastated.

Later on, I asked Mom more than once if Dad loved me. It was not a rhetorical question.

My parents' grave in Elmira, NY

The funeral was a closed-casket affair at our lifeless, gothic stone church, which just added to the sense of an irreparable separation.

I learned to tie a necktie that day. Someone instructed me that I was now the man of the family. No one should ever tell a 9-year-old that. It meant that I couldn't cry, and that I inherited some vague, undefined – and impossible – adult responsibilities.

My sister Robin, then 12, was as stricken as I. We didn't talk about it much – it was just too painful, and no one prompted us. Also sensitive, but kinder and more considerate, Robin suffered mostly in silence. A few years later, she went off to Emma Willard to boarding preparatory school, as much to escape the household sadness and dysfunction, as to get a superb education.

Always bright and perceptive, Robin figured out that Dad was going to die without being told. She confronted Mom who swore her to secrecy.

Years later I asked Mom why she hid all of that from me. She replied that Dad's doctor knew he was going to die that night. When she and Dad were at various cancer hospitals, she witnessed the struggle of patients dying in respiratory distress and wanted to spare us that. As they say, no good deed goes unpunished.

Robin and me during happy times in Elmira, NY

It's hard to remember what I thought, but not what I felt, which was sad and abandoned. I was now the only male in a family of women. There were no other father figures: my paternal grandfather was distant and lacked palpable affection. My great uncle on my mother's side was kind and solicitous, but he lived far away and had no children of his own (and no parenting experience).

Acting out in school, I found distraction and attention in mischief and trouble. If I was missing attention from one parent, I was sure to get it from the remaining one – and from anyone else I could.

I was invited to sleepovers; to go fishing; or to spend a few days at the Finger Lakes, often by family friends who wanted to distract me with kindness or give Mom a break. However, there was no balm in Gilead, and it was futile to try to fill the hole, or even to cover it over.

For many years after Dad's death, I had a recurring nightmare. I would open a closet and my father, now a ghoul, would emerge to punish me. I was the bad child and deserved it.

In the apotheosis of nightmares, I was in the empty attic of my grandfather's Riverdale house; the wooden floor darkly polished, with black doors all around. It was an enormous, cold room that signified death itself. One of the doors opened up and my father's dark spirit emerged and rose, filling the entire attic – and me with dread and terror.

Years later when I was in college, I received a miraculous gift. I had the most vivid dream. My father and I spoke to each other like long-lost friends. He gave me his blessing. It healed my soul and spirit and gave me new peace. It was as real as it needed to be.

I still mourn that I didn't have the opportunity to know him as an adult; that he didn't get to know and enjoy his grandchildren. Part of the loss is that so much of his brief life will always be a mystery.

Devoid of a paternal role model, I learned about fatherhood from my wife Michelle and my children. The joy and engagement of parenthood helped me to see my own father in a different way and to heal some of the grief surrounding him.

Reflection: I rarely talked about my father and his death, although I needed to. Mere mention of him or his death would bring tears – sometimes subtle, sometimes not. The pain is like an embedded splinter: it might be covered up by new skin, but it is still sore and sensitive to the touch.

Young children who lose a parent to death seem especially disadvantaged. For my mother – and surely for most other surviving parents – the loss is life-changing apart from the grief. The role of a father was forced upon my mother: someone had to wield the belt and also make a living. It is easy to understand how a child's emotional needs get lost in the fray.

Betsy, an Elmira friend from my old neighborhood, recently talked about losing her mother to cancer a year or two before my father died. Her family struggled with the loss and upheaval as well. She remembered that she wanted to reach out and comfort me after learning of Dad's death, but she did not know how and did not have the words – after all, we were only nine or ten. Besides our age and the cultural taboos, the gender difference may have provided an additional obstacle for her.

When I recall the other children who lost parents while in elementary school, each was devastated by the loss, and struggled with the changes to family dynamics. Their grief was persistent, measured in years.

Matt, a friend in sixth grade, was one of five or six siblings. His family included me in family activities after Dad died. One day Matt went home from school to discover that his mother had asphyxiated herself in the garage. I do not recall what happened afterwards to Matt or his family, and we lost touch.

Decades later, I located him in Connecticut, and we talked by phone. He revealed that every one of his siblings became alcoholics or had other severe emotional problems post-suicide.

In my experience and observation, the notion that children can just "get over it" without professional assistance is myopic, wishful thinking – or simply wrong.

Epiphany Before Banishment

When I was in eighth grade, a buddy named Carl sold me a small amount of marijuana to try. That satisfied one curiosity, but he then replaced it with another.

Carl piqued my interest by telling me that he attended a "class" that had – among other esoteric secrets – a Divine pattern that determined the underlying structure and function of the entire universe, and other esoteric claims. He invited me to check it out. Being the ever-curious kid who read the World Book Encyclopedia for fun, I went along.

Carl and his family were members of a cult that purported to be a "Bible study group" and a "religious and scientific research organization." Each meeting was two hours of a lecture format. I was mesmerized by their doctrines and dogma, and I was welcomed into the group right away. They became my new family.

"Class" became a central focus of my life. They claimed that only they had the truth, and what's more, that the world was going to end. Soon. Guess who would be saved, and who wouldn't?

The group conducted weekly meetings in Elmira, but members would drive to other cities and towns in New York to attend similar classes hosted by other branches. I attended whenever I could, and I spent my spare time at the homes of the other "classmates."

Now freshly immersed in the "truth," it was my responsibility to proselytize to get others to attend the lectures. I was an obedient student, and Mom became deeply concerned.

At some point – probably before I had joined the cult – Mom had decided that I was going to "go away" to boarding school, courtesy of my grandfather. And now it was an imperative, to separate me from the group. She told me I needed to be with "other men" and that I needed to have a better education. I loved my friends in public school in Elmira, and I had no desire to be sent elsewhere.

We visited a few schools in New England, and I settled on Taft, then an all-male boarding school. I hated it. Most of the other kids were well to do. They might be going to Switzerland to ski during Christmas break, while I was trying to navigate the trains and busses to get back to blue-collar Elmira. We had to wear jackets and ties to class. And there were no girls the first year, although the school soon became coed.

I didn't adapt. I missed my cult family, my Elmira friends, and the twins.

To the cult I was exiled in Babylon – there was no branch Bible school anywhere nearby. Most of the money I had ended up in the pay phones calling others in the group, especially Mitch, the "Dean" of the class. I would talk until I ran out of change or called collect.

I was depressed. I learned to play the blues harmonica and would wander the sports fields above the campus at night, either playing the blues or walking in sadness, prayer and meditation, longing to be home or with my cult family. The campus below, with its shining lights, felt like a prison.

I was obsessed with God and the group's teachings. During my freshman year I stayed in my dorm room to read the Bible or the group's literature, while others watched a first-run Saturday night movie.

I engaged in ritual, obsessive-compulsive behaviors such as making certain that my shoes were in the proper position before sleeping; counting stairs and steps; or washing my hands too much. It was an attempt to have complete control over something.

The Taft School, Watertown, CT

During my adolescent mood swings, I might start a day in particular distress, concerned that it might well be a permanent state of mind.

On long breaks I would take a train to Grand Central, and walk down 42nd street to the Port Authority, where I would transfer to a bus for the long ride home to Elmira. During my trek across New York, I was invariably accosted by men who would try to entice me with a promise of five dollars for engaging in unspeakable acts.

New York in the 70s felt cold, inhospitable and dangerous. Yet once in the midst of that Babylon, I had a remarkable, mystical experience – my own "miracle" on 42nd Street.

While walking outside of Grand Central, I experienced a brief change of consciousness. The city landscape faded a bit, and I became acutely aware of everyone within my immediate vicinity. My heart suddenly opened, I felt an intense and inexplicable love and kinship with everyone I saw. I became aware that people were responding with stares and some smiles. For a few fleeting moments, I basked in the light, never to forget the experience nor the feeling.

I felt on fire. Like a 4th of July sparkler, the effervescent light burned briefly and bright, and set my heart aglow.

It was one of those ephemeral, mystical things that could not be repeated at will, but worth yearning for. I intuitively understood how we are all connected in the spirit; a lesson to be repeated later, sometimes with grief.

Reflection: I spoke to my Taft teachers and advisors about my distress and depression. Although they were attentive and kind, the prevailing advice for my sadness and depression was to "tough it out" – a familiar prescription. Students were rarely referred for counseling, and antidepressant options were few and seldom dispensed.

I realize now that my depression then was a form of grief. I was forcibly separated from my friends and loved ones, and powerless to change the status quo. My sadness was stifling and unrelenting, but unlike death, it was situational and lasted four years.

I waited a few decades before I attended any high school reunions, which were surprisingly gratifying. I discovered that many of my peers were also miserable at Taft. I made new, stronger bonds with several classmates. Some of the affinity was due, no doubt, to having the shared experience or perception of "being in the trenches" together. Eventually I came to regard my Taft experience with gratitude for the education and the friendships, but it was a gradual shift.

"The Undoing"

My wife Michelle and I enjoyed "The Undoing," an exotic whodunit short series starring Nicole Kidman and Hugh Grant. Grant's family's dissolution begins with the tragic death of his younger sister, who was struck and killed by a car. (Bier, 2020)

Sometimes life imitates art; and sometimes art imitates life.

2020 marked the 39th anniversary of the death of my baby sister Lisa. In the twinkling of an eye, my family unraveled. My mother lost her faith: she thought her young widowhood would give her a respite from more personal tragedy. Lisa's twin sister Suzy was hospitalized at Ridgeview, a mental health facility. The complicated and difficult rest, as they say – is history.

Lisa and me outside of Mom's Atlanta condo, ca. 1981

We moved to Atlanta after my first year at Taft, Mom decided that Elmira didn't offer good prospects for remarriage, and she needed a change of venue. Running away was her pattern for dealing with adversity, and Atlanta offered a fresh start. She knew no one there.

Our family lived in a condo on Clairmont Road. The twins worked at the Book Nook a few blocks away, before they were old enough to get a job permit. At about age 14 or so, Suzy began to manifest signs of anorexia nervosa.

One night while coming home from the Book Nook, Lisa crossed Clairmont Road without her glasses, and was struck and killed by a passing car. Suzy witnessed the aftermath. She was sixteen.

I was working late at a job in Chamblee and shared a drab prefab WWII house with a church choir director. I got a phone call at work from a family friend — "Lisa was in an accident and I needed to go to the hospital." I did not know that it meant that she had already died.

Later that night, I played a Ralph Towner ballad, "Beneath an Evening Sky," over and over again on the phonograph, while I drank until I blacked out. I have no clue how I drove a few miles to my bleak rented room. (Towner, 1987)

My family's pain was like shared second-degree burns. Suzy had become distant and disconnected, increasingly so. I was chosen to go to the funeral home and the cemetery to make the final arrangements. Did I want the $5,000 basic white casket, or the polished cherry mahogany one for $9,000? Everything about it was horrid.

Suzy wanted Lisa to be buried nearby in the Decatur Cemetery. However, there was a problem: they sold plots only in pairs. My grieving mother thought it was a bad omen and could not contemplate the loss of the other twin. The cemetery was dead set against breaking up the real estate, so my older friend Virgil Hartley visited the cemetery's office and somehow convinced them to make an exception.

The funeral at St. Bartholomew's was excruciating and interminable. Suzy got up to speak about her missing half, wearing the jean jacket that Lisa wore when she died.

I faded from the Episcopalian service. I could have been atop a tall, ancient Mayan pyramid; strapped onto a stone altar. The priest raised the sharpened stone above his head, and I felt the tear of flesh and the splinter of bone. I was conscious of the shearing of every muscle and fiber as he ripped my heart from my chest, still beating.

I wanted to die. My anxiety went through the roof and up the steeple, but my soul wouldn't follow. There was no release and no relief.

I was visited by a black rage that I had never experienced. It was overpowering and completely blinding. I viscerally understood how people could commit murder in a fit of fulminant anger, and it terrified me. Not so much that I would actually kill someone; but that so depthless a rage existed within my soul. I tore into my girlfriend for not being present and supportive. I am surprised that she didn't leave me.

The next few days, weeks and months were surreal. Suzy was physically wasting away and showing unmistakable signs of serious mental illness. Her psychiatrist committed her to the Ridgeview Institute, a mental health hospital. She was strip-searched daily and put on suicide watch, adding to her trauma. She was so traumatized by the experience that she figured out how to act to get released, but her decline continued. Eventually she was hospitalized for the anorexia, and in grave danger. I was furious. How could she do this? Hadn't Mom suffered enough?

After her hospitalization, Suzy eventually regained her composure, overcame her anorexia, and built an outstanding and lucrative real estate career. She also lived a life of incredible compassion, generosity, and kindness to others. She had the biggest heart of anyone I had ever met, without hyperbole.

I was not very good at tending to the needs of my broken family; my own wounds kept my attention. I drank a lot and fell into a year or more of depression. My mother got some solace from a therapy group for grieving parents, but I was unaware of options for myself.

I visited Suzy's psychiatrist for a few sessions, but he provided scant relief. I was on my own once again.

Suzy often talked about her twin and her own pain, but my mother, sister and I generally avoided sharing our feelings and talking about Lisa. It was just too painful. That only drove the pain deeper, to cry for eventual expression and release.

Life goes on somehow and nonetheless. Intuitive people could sense my deep inner sadness, in spite of my attempts to be jovial and "normal." They almost uniformly described it as a veil upon my heart, a kind of spiritual marker of heart trauma.

Reflection: The shock of a surprise death causes intense and long-lasting sorrow. Obviously, the grief engendered by the quiet passing of an elderly friend or relative is almost a totally different sort from a loss without warning. The death of a child may be in a separate category by itself; surely nothing is more tragic for a parent. The sudden loss of a sibling – especially one whom I "parented" in some respects – is comparably devastating.

My grief brought depression. I drank and self-medicated to deal with the pain. An employee at the firm where I worked had a huge cache of Valium, which she shared with me. Numbing didn't help or resolve the underlying pain.

In retrospect, I am sure that competent and effective psychotherapy would have helped perhaps to shorten the arc of grief. It also might have better addressed the self-destructive behaviors that followed the losses.

Disinheritance

The accumulation of money did not seem very important to my mother's side of the family – probably because they never had very much of it.

In contrast, it seemed the raison d'etre for most of my father's relatives.

My grandfather Louis Yaeger was born in Austria at the fin de siècle. He, along with his sisters and two brothers, emigrated to New York City. Louis grew up on the Lower East Side and joined a gang. He had the gang's insignia tattoo hidden in an armpit.

Louis stole milk and other food to help feed his family. Later on he went to Columbia University and graduated as a member of Phi Beta Kappa.

He played the stock market and built a sizable fortune, which he lost in the crash of 1929. Undeterred, Louis started anew and built a considerable fortune in the 1950s. He never told his wife that he was rich. She regularly took a train from Riverdale to New York City to search for low priced groceries and bargains.

My grandmother Libby died of cancer when I was four. Louis remarried to Sylvia "Betty" Horne. Betty was notorious for compelling her daughter, who became the actress Tina Louise, to testify as a child in a divorce proceeding – something that was "not done" in those days. She was a complicated woman, sometimes randomly thoughtful and generous, but also a terror to the domestics and cooks she employed, and occasionally to others on a whim. She had no compunction about spending Louis' money, which he otherwise hoarded. I know of no charity he supported during his life.

In many ways, my grandfather was "larger than life," a Horatio Alger figure with enough drama and eccentricities for a compelling biography or novel.

I spent the summer of my 18th year at his estate in Greenwich – one of three properties, which included a two-story New York City apartment at 955 Fifth Avenue and a huge Florida complex that spanned from the Atlantic Ocean to the inter-coastal waterway. Mar a Lago (now owned by Donald Trump) was nearly next door.

Even when close, my grandfather remained a cipher. He was a loner and introvert who abhorred small talk, working late into the night researching investments. Louis loved Mozart and Shakespeare, whom he quoted often and at length.

My grandfather was distant, sometimes cold, and no substitute for my father. I think he liked me – but it was hard to be sure. He lacked outward natural affection that most grandchildren take for granted.

Somehow my father and he became estranged, but he doted upon my Aunt Judith, my father's only sibling. I never learned what might have caused the rift, but my father consciously lived in his shadow.

When Louis died in 1981, he left almost all of his fortune to Judith. I estimate that his estate was worth somewhere between $300 - $400 million, but the amount was never disclosed, because Judith compelled the court to make it a secret.

The will had a couple of codicils. The last one left his grandchildren $100K each. Rumor had it that it was coerced; the signature on it bore no apparent likeness to his signature on the other documents.

After my father died, one might expect that the only son of an only son – the exclusive heir to the family name – might inherit something more substantial. Later, a lawyer explained that had the grandchildren not been specifically named, we would have had grounds for challenging the entire will. My immediate family believed that Judith knew this as well, and hence the final codicil. Louis left no funds or provision to support my mother, a widow with a duty to raise his grandchildren.

My immediate family was essentially disinherited.

After my sister Lisa died, Judith petitioned the court to try to reclaim Lisa's portion, which would otherwise be distributed among her siblings. Apparently $300 million was not enough. Even the presiding judge called her out for her rapacity.

Oddly perhaps, my naïve hope of a normal and loving relationship with my grandfather was more important to me than his money. The wealth he accumulated was never mine to begin with, so I did not regard is as a true loss.

Nonetheless, my grandfather's callousness hurt. The behind-the-scenes machinations and monstrous avarice of my Aunt Judith, was – and remains – beyond my comprehension.

My aunt and I haven't spoken since the early 80s, and neither have I had contact with my two cousins since. They may all be dead to me, but there is no grief.

A Graceful Exit

My maternal grandmother's attitude towards death – as well as the gentle circumstances of her passing – made grief almost self-indulgent.

Nana (my maternal grandmother) came from Alsace in the early 1900s with her siblings and mother. Her father stayed behind, for reasons we never knew. She married an engaging salesman with the Herald Tribune, who got into trouble with booze. At some point, she made him go to an asylum to dry out. He died in their bed the night he came home. This occurred in the midst of the Great Depression. She never remarried, and so far as I know, never courted again or had suitors.

Nana commuted to work in New York City and earned enough to put her children through college. Her son James (Willie) died in college from Guillian-Barre syndrome, a rare disease.

Nana lived alone for decades in an apartment on the "wrong side of the tracks" in Bronxville, NY. She was partial to men, and having lost all of the ones she loved, she doted upon me.

Although she and my mother did not get along well, she made a considerable effort to be present in her grandchildren's lives. She felt that Mom drank too much and abandoned Suzy during her time of greatest need – and she was right. Nana collected grudges and hurts and kept them. If she was on your side, you had no greater champion, but if not, heaven help you.

My sisters were second-class citizens. Once she offered to give me ten thousand dollars, for no apparent reason. This offer came from a lady with a reputation for extreme frugality, someone who recycled old bits of soap and reused aluminum foil and plastic. I gently declined her gift as unfair and hurtful to the others.

Regular visits to Bronxville to see her were mandatory, even as adults. And so were Sunday telephone calls.

When visiting, we would talk for hours. She walked every day, often up the hill to the train station and Baskin Robbins in town for ice cream, or to a nearby park. I recall one trek together; our hands found each other's. It felt a little awkward at first – after all, I was a self-conscious teen. Her hands were wrinkled and dry, but warm. That simple gesture made me meditate upon her isolation; the men she loved and lost; and how basic is our need for simple affection.

Nana occasionally drove to Watertown, CT from Bronxville in her ugly green Dodge Dart, to spend the better part of a day with me at Taft. She always brought homemade applesauce, pound cake, and a chicken sandwich, all made with love.

Sometimes she forgot and called me "Willie." As she aged she suffered from creeping decrepitude: her deafness worsened and her vision degenerated, but her mind was always sharp. Although she never went further in education than high school, she managed the library for a Madison Avenue advertising agency and was the best-read person I knew. She completed the Sunday New York Times crossword puzzle almost every week.

Nana had a well-developed sense of ethics, which she shared with me, and I largely adopted. Apart from Mom, she was my most influential relative.

In her 80s, she accepted the idea of her eventual death, almost welcoming it. She would often refer to herself as "these tired old bones."

I was appointed as the executor of her will. I don't recall the exact circumstances, but we visited her delightful old attorney to discuss it. She planned everything, including organizing her financial records to make the administration of her will easier.

Mom's nuclear family in the late 1920s

She left Bronxville and spent the last few years of her life at Pennswood Village, a Quaker retirement community in Bucks County, PA. It was adjacent to the George School, a private high school that her son Willie attended before Hamilton. She was content in her small apartment and enjoyed socializing.

Now in her 90s, she went with a small group of residents to a theatre to watch "The Secret Garden." She suffered a heart attack during the film but chose to ignore it. Later, she explained that she was more interested in seeing the end of the movie than attending to her own distress. That's who she was.

Her condition deteriorated rapidly. My sister Suzy flew to Pennsylvania to be with her during her transition. In retrospect, I don't know why I didn't accompany her.

During her service, I delivered a heart-felt eulogy. Nana had lived a long, healthy life on her own terms, and she also left on them too. In a final act of independence kept hidden from the family, she had donated her body to medical science to avoid the effort and expense of a full funeral.

Reflection: I miss my grandmother and think of her often. She was a very powerful woman in her own right, a good and loyal friend as well as a loving influence. She lived a full, if difficult life, but it was on her own terms – at least of the things that she could control. I wonder what she would have accomplished if she had been born a half century later.

It's hard to harbor deep grief or sadness over the natural end to a life well lived. Gratitude fits better. As Helen Keller (1929) observed:

What we have once enjoyed
we can never lose.
All that we love deeply
becomes a part of us.

And so I carry on her legacy, both in my DNA and my heart.

Reconciliation

My mother Nancy was what people used to call "a character." She was quirky and intuitive, talented in the arts and very perceptive. She was an optimistic romantic who hated to be bored.

Mom met my father while she was a student at Elmira College. They fell madly in love and had a lot of fun together, as well as with their crowd of friends in Elmira.

My parents lost their first child. Within the next nine months, my mother's only brother died suddenly at college. My sister Robin was born next, and I arrived two years later.

My father was transferred to Scarsdale, NY for a few years, and it was a very unhappy time – probably for both of them. The town was near both sets of in-laws, who regularly interfered with their lives without invitation. Mom also worried that Dad was having an affair in the city, and she suffered what she termed a "nervous breakdown."

There is an old Southern aphorism: "if mama ain't happy, ain't nobody happy."

After a few years, it was back to Elmira where she enjoyed being a mother, housewife, dinner party hostess, and community volunteer — typical roles for a middle-class woman of that era. She "got her groove back" far from Westchester County and the relatives.

Mom in Barbados

In childhood, I remember cuddling with Mom in a rocking chair, but she wasn't very "huggy" — especially as we grew. Notably, if you were sick, you always got special care and attention. Although she didn't always express it, her maternal love was steadfast.

She shared her passion for literature, the arts, and culture. My mother also taught us manners, and instilled compassion and a sense of decency and fair play in all of her children. She didn't always succeed: years of forced piano and dancing lessons were wasted on me.

Understandably, my father's death changed her. After he died, she was certain that no one else could make her as happy, and her optimism began to wane.

Now a widow in her 30s with four small children, she took on both parental roles out of necessity. We used to call her "The Sarge," for issuing constant orders, a persona she said she never liked. Nonetheless, it persisted after we were adults.

I was a quirky, curious, and mischievous kid, and Mom didn't quite know what to do with me. I launched rockets from the basement and made bombs; blew the house's main fuse with my experiments; and roamed the quiet streets of Elmira with my friends, looking for excitement and trouble. I went to the emergency room with alcohol poisoning, and again when a UV phosphor compound I was making on the stove blew up and gave me second-degree burns.

I'm sure the last straw was when I joined the cult as a teen. Mom couldn't reach me and I began to view her as an enemy separating me from the group. She was terrified of their grip on me, and we sparked often.

When I was about 18, I had an epiphany. I asked Mom, "You really don't enjoy fighting, do you?" It became a turning point in our relationship, and we became friends. We talked a lot, saw movies together, and shared cocktail hours and cigarettes. I remember helping her walk home from a neighborhood party where she was introduced to margaritas. She was smashed, and we laughed about it as we stumbled home arm in arm.

Lisa's death changed everything.

As Suzy became more despondent and mentally ill, Mom checked out. She moved to Barbados for her own healing and sanity, as a newcomer trying to start afresh once more.

My grandmother was angry that Mom abandoned Suzy during a very critical and needy time, and never got over it. Many of Mom's friends also were appalled. Robin and I realized that our devastated parent was emotionally fragile and lacked the strength to deal with Suzy and her problems. Her exodus was from desperation.

We stayed in touch, but like most things, the relationship was on her terms. We would visit from time to time, and she would dote on us while we were there. It was hard to maintain a healthy relationship at a distance, and ours languished.

Mom eventually moved back to the Atlanta area after Robin married and had a child. She bought a little bungalow in Decatur and hosted her friends for dinner and cocktail parties like before, but something had changed. She had become more critical and negative, which alienated her from some of her old friends. I used to say about Mom's Weltanschauung that, "not only was the glass half-empty; the glass was dirty, too."

My mother aired her opinions and criticisms as she saw fit, without much regard for people's reactions to them. Thus, her comments that I "looked tired," "was working too much," "had dark circles under my eyes," or "didn't exercise enough" were constant refrains. She pointed out other people's flaws, culinary deficiencies, and other petty grievances. It made her company less fun and strained our relationship.

When I was single, Mom would visit my apartment or condo and rearrange the furniture, or cross some other personal boundary: apparently she forgot how her own mother's intrusions made her feel.

Robin and her family moved to Durham, and Mom followed later on.

One day Mom's colon ruptured, and she developed peritonitis. She was intubated on a ventilator and had multiple surgeries – including a colostomy, which mortified her. She was a proud woman who did not suffer this indignity in stride.

My sisters and I took turns caring for her. My turn didn't go well. She resented her dependency and my presence. She was angry and sick and as she often explained, the ones you love carry the burden of that. I left saddened that it did not bring us closer.

She had corrective surgery for the colostomy but had trouble with her bowels thereafter. Apparently being on a ventilator damaged her lungs, causing COPD. Her health was declining, so she joined a senior retirement community.

It was a six- or seven-hour drive from Atlanta to Durham, and I visited when I could, despite mixed feelings. I would initially be optimistic, only to have them deflated when Mom's first words to me might be, "You look terrible." She was physically and spiritually broken, embittered and angry as ever.

She knew she was going to die. Just before she passed, we had an amazing long phone call. We apologized to each other for various hurts and deficiencies and expressed our love and mutual admiration.

Soon after she died, instead of being distraught, I sensed peace and connection where both had been missing or broken.

Reflection: Ironically, my reaction to Mom's expected death was not what I had anticipated. Instead of being overwhelmed by grief, I experienced tranquility and balance from having finally achieved reconciliation and a release from the burdens of doubt, want and resentment. Although rekindling of our relationship was at the very end, it was a bright, healing flame that continues to glow.

There is solace in knowing that her passing brought release from the chronic suffering and angst that defined her last days.

Oddly, my sadness was greater at times when I contemplated her death without the benefit of resolution or closure. I recall one dark winter night's drive to Durham, being summoned to the hospital for an assumed deathwatch. It was during a meteor shower. I stopped at an unlit rest area and watched a metaphor of life itself: brief trajectories of the tiny orbs of light fading into darkness. I was physically cold and felt a kind of existential loneliness – fearing that death might cheat me once more.

I am sad that my mother is gone. Her parting gift to me brought wholeness; not distress or emotional poverty. I can do nothing more than miss her, acknowledging gratitude for the gift of life, and for all of the love shared along the way.

My Beautiful Sister

Suzy had the good fortune to inherit her appearance from my mother's side of the family. Diminutive and slender, she had beautiful blue eyes and a radiant smile, and a wicked, infectious laugh. She cultivated her appearance and took good care of herself, except for a perennial obsession with food associated with anorexia.

Suzy occasionally complained that she did not think she was as bright as her older siblings, but that is simply untrue. Her intelligence was razor-sharp. But perhaps more importantly, she benefited from an "emotional I.Q." that was astounding. She had my mother's gift of intuition and "people smarts" – and then some.

As children, Suzy and her twin were exceptional. Not in the traditional notions of academic excellence or precociousness, but in their reflexive kindness, consideration, and generosity. They would assist any stranger, as well as any friend or relative in need. And often just because.

As teens, they pooled their allowances to anonymously buy and deliver groceries for people struggling in the neighborhood. After Lisa died, Suzy expanded her benevolence, a tribute to her other half.

Suzy with Lizzie

Around 2000, Suzy volunteered to work with at-risk infants and toddlers at a shelter called My House in midtown Atlanta. There she bonded with Lizzie, a profoundly physically and mentally challenged child of a crack addict. She became like a surrogate parent and tried to adopt her.

The odds were against her as a single parent. Even so, she initiated a long legal fight to try to gain custody. The contest exhausted her physical energy, her finances, and ultimately her spirit. A judge granted her limited visitation rights, against long odds. Nonetheless, she was dissatisfied.

My mother's death in 2013 was a huge blow, and it precipitated a deep depression. They were co-dependent and often sparked, but they remained extremely close.

Suzy had been prescribed a plethora of medications including Xanax, Ritalin, and various antidepressants, which she took concomitantly. The drugs affected her ability to focus and concentrate, and she was worried that she was losing her mind and would be unable to continue her very successful real estate career, and thus her ability to support herself and provide for Lizzie.

My sister Robin and I were deeply concerned, but powerless to counteract the gravity of her depression. We had many phone conversations trying to figure out what to do. Suzy said that if we had her committed again to a place like Ridgeview, she would take her life. It was no idle threat.

We steered her to medical doctors; different psychiatrists; and any resources that we could think of. Adjusting her medications did not seem to help. I sent her some funds to take a much-needed vacation and rest.

A week or so before her death, I held her close and smelled her hair. I could still smell my baby sister, but this time it was tinged with fear, sadness, and resignation.

In her suicide note, she said that the trigger event was a lawsuit for about $4800 she received that morning from a pettifogger that she employed on the custody case. He had sexually harassed her and served her badly as a lawyer. I called him later and made sure he understood his role in her death.

Assuming she did not want to defile her lovely house, she took several family pictures, along with some of her medications and some alcohol, and consumed them in a Hampton Inn Hotel room located about a mile from her house. Room service found her lifeless body in the morning of December 13, which was a week after the anniversary of Lisa's death.

The next day I received a cold call at work from the Brookhaven police department, notifying me of her death. I yelled — loud and long.

It was Wednesday. I had enrolled in Georgia State's Master of Public Health program and had the final exam in epidemiology the night before. I had not spoken to Suzy for several days: I was deep in study.

It later occurred to me that she had deliberately postponed her suicide until after I had taken the final, knowing how important it was to me. I also discovered that Suzy had changed her executor at the very last, from a dear friend with two small children, to a woman with none. She was considerate and thoughtful to the end, which – considering the depth of her sadness and depression – was remarkable.

She was always that.

A few days later, I received a letter from her with a refund of the vacation check, which she must have dropped into the mail before she went to the hotel. I couldn't read the note then, so I set it aside. When I eventually did, I sobbed as it tore my heart and set it aflame. It was unbearable in its loving kindness, which she somehow managed in the midst of her considerable, final suffering. Utterly devastated, I stuck it somewhere I now can't recall. I need to find it. When I do, I hope that I will be able to cherish the message and the love that penned it.

I never thought we would have to do an encore at St. Bartholomew's. I thought that I would predecease her, and she would say some words at my own funeral. Saying goodbye to the remaining twin was an untenable, cruel twist of fate.

There hadn't been much public announcement of the funeral, but the church was packed. Many had not learned of her death beforehand. Friends and co-workers from across the county attended. I was prepared for the worst, but I felt none of the overpowering anxiety that vexed me during Lisa's service. I was now a regular meditator, and I used the acquired skills to control my breathing and focus. It worked, thank God.

Suzy's best friend Lisa McDuffie delivered a brilliant, heart-felt, and stirring eulogy.

We had a small, private burial service. Against my mother's wishes – and likely without her knowledge, Suzy had purchased a burial plot in the Decatur Cemetery, as close to Lisa's as she could find. They were somewhat together, at last.

I was the unofficial officiant and held my composure as well as I could.

Reflection: When death comes unexpectedly, it forces a kind of autopilot mode. You do what you must to get through the requisites, often half-dazed and numb.

When the required funereal duties are completed, life goes on, but not as before. There is a change of consciousness, as if a weighted blanket is draped over your soul; or gauze that obscures joy, imparting sepia tones to life's once vibrant colors.

Suzy's graveside service at the Decatur Cemetery

Grief has been described as having stages that include denial, anger, bargaining, depression and acceptance. Notably, they are the same hallmarks of one's consciousness of impending death. When we recognize these processes within our painful predicaments, they seem less random and lose some of their power.

My depression was stubborn and persistent. For two years following Suzy's death, I felt grief's firm grasp. Therapy helped immensely. People could see that I was sad, and I couldn't pretend otherwise – I was unable to "fake it until you make it."

Evidently, you are not done with grief until it is done with you. It cannot be rushed. Lingering grief has its own time and process. You are captive to an arrangement that you never wanted, agreed to, or signed up for. The contract isn't for perpetuity. Someday it will end or at least become bearable. The end of mine felt miraculous.

One night I simply dreamed that I could be happy again. About a week later, the grief lifted – it was gone. My family and friends noticed immediately. Many told me, "you're not grieving any more!" – like I'd just surfaced after swimming under water for two years. It was a profound, welcomed renewal. I later understood that the dream was my subconscious telling me I was ready.

Suzy Postscript

Suzy was able to connect with people to a degree and at a depth that was remarkable. For as long as her phone was active after her death, I would get calls from people from all over the country, hoping to contact her. When I intercepted those calls and spoke to them – relaying the bad news – they might share stories of having met her only briefly, but that the connection became a touchstone in their own lives.

For example, she befriended a nurse who assisted our mother when she was in the ICU more than a decade ago. The woman spoke to Suzy about her own problems, and Suzy called her religiously about every 6 months to check on her.

This scenario recurred again and again, and I came to realize what a profound impact her care and empathy had on those who crossed her path.

I've wanted to emulate and honor that. Not necessarily with those she knew, but with those in my own circle. It was and is a daunting task; she was so much better at it than I could possibly seem to manage.

• • •

Maybe a year or two after her death, I was at a Starbuck's drive-through, located near my sister's house, when a woman in the car ahead randomly paid for my coffee. It was something that Suzy, also a donor of kindness to random strangers, would have done. I was stunned and teary.

Missing my sister, I drove by her empty house blocks away before going home. Her lovely home was dark and sad. It had been her sanctuary as well as her asylum, and her "vibe" was too strong for me to bear. My family knew and saved me the pain of having to organize and pack up her things there.

About a year later, I drove back again, and saw several people in her living room. The light inside was bright and there was artwork and activity. I realized that Suzy had moved on, and I hoped that I could too.

With a Little Help from My Friends

My journey to the return of any semblance of wholeness following Suzy's suicide would have been impossible without the caring and loving support of friends, family, and a gifted therapist.

My wife and children provided ample latitude to grieve. Their concern about my state of mind was tempered with kindness and respect, never patronizing. If I didn't want to celebrate Christmas the following year, they went along.

I often "checked out" from work. Andy – more of a brother than a key employee – kept things on track and put up with me when my moods were dark or foul. He went with me to the police station to try to reclaim Suzy's car. Throughout two difficult years, he tended to me like a lost sheep, always keeping my best interests at heart, even when I had no clue what those might have been. You can't ask for that: it comes from the heart.

Friends of Suzy's kept in touch and checked on my welfare. I chat often with Lisa McDuffie, who had tried harder than anyone to help Suzy in her distress. Her friendship is a gift to me.

A business associate of Suzy's and a fraternity brother of mine (from a younger class) invites me out to lunch regularly. It was a new connection for me, and I have been touched by his kindness, selflessness, and generosity (no wonder Suzy had a crush on him).

From the neighborhood detective who invited me to go hunting at his farm in south Georgia, to time spent in the company of caring others, there are too many to mention. All of them made a difference, individually and collectively. Grieving and chatting and laughing is good medicine.

I have been participating in a group meditation practice since 2000. My meditation leader and teacher is a practicing psychologist.

Becky is unusually gifted and perceptive, one of the most caring and loving people I know. She departed from the usual focus of her counseling and provided marvelously effective therapy for my grief. The difference between the "therapy" I received after Lisa died, versus what I experienced with Becky are on two ends of the spectrum. Becky's ministrations were integral to my healing.

My friendships with some of Suzy's other friends have deepened and matured. We're able to look back now and talk about the dysfunctional parts of her lovely soul: to see her now more as she was, than as we wanted her to be.

My wife Michelle and I and a few of Suzy's "besties" got together for an impromptu dinner and to share memories when our grief was fresh. Our focus was to dwell on the funny and quirky things, recalling the things we loved about her.

A year or two later, we joined a smaller group of her friends for dinner. This time we gave a bit more voice to the other side of the ledger – to share how we could not contain the grief and terror and depression that Suzy felt towards the end of her life, that spilled into our own.

Each had earnestly tried to get her to help and safety, but her ultimate trajectory was as certain as a helicopter that had lost its prop. The tragedy is that her own goodness could not save her from the intense and unmanageable forces she suffered.

The evening was bittersweet, but healing. While we were casual acquaintances before, what we could share made us feel like kin. How kind and generous of them to enclose me in their circle.

An Unexpected Gift

The paradox of loss is that you can gain from it.

A heart that has been wounded by tragedy is also an open heart. It can bring a new awareness – or a potent reminder – that we are all connected in our sorrows and our sufferings. We sense it now in the strangers that we meet. We are more acutely aware of sadness not only in our lives - but in the lives of others. It underscores the value of those who we love; and presses us to enlarge that community. We hold our loved ones closer, and we are better for it.

After my sister's suicide, I felt like a tuning fork or a "Geiger counter" for emotional pain and distress. Complete strangers would approach me and tell me about their own sorrows, apropos of nothing in particular. Misery may not love company, but it seeks it.

Once, when ordering a pizza, a cook picked me out of the line of customers to tell me about his brother in the VA hospital, in detail. It was both intimate and matter of fact, and I consoled him as best as I could from the queue line. That I was chosen to hear his story didn't feel random to me.

In my meditation class, other meditators picked up on my sadness, as I did on theirs. They also sensed when the sorrow lifted.

Grief's hypersensitivity manifested in other ways. I have always been moved by emotional scenes in drama, romance, and music; apt to tear up in a theatre, concert hall, or TV room. When you are grieving the threshold is lowered and little things that might have gone unnoticed before trigger reactions that may be puzzling or uncomfortable to others present. Scenes from a movie, or any random trigger may bring the tears.

Joe Biden said, "There will come a day, I promise you and your parents, as well, when the thought of your son or daughter or your husband or wife brings a smile to your lips before it brings a tear to your eye. It will happen."

It is a paradox. I experience both.

In the meantime, I am grateful for the newfound hypersensitivity; a greater sense of connection with people, and feelings of a shared human destiny. I suppose that this evolutionary process began with Nana's death, subtle at first.

The forging of a Japanese sword may serve as a metaphor. After repeated rounds of fire, annealing, and quenching, the very character of the metal changes into something finer, able to penetrate soft tissue to the bone beneath.

There may be some hidden "cost." I had participated in a men's breakfast group since 2000. One or more in my cohort remarked that a lot of my usual silliness and irreverence had gone missing. I changed. Or perhaps it is better to say that it changed me.

Grief can be a "gift" that keeps on giving. Maybe like the underwear and socks you got for Christmas; it isn't what you wanted, but it's something that you needed.

Goodnight, Irene

Those of us who are lucky or blessed can count the benefit of more than one mother in our lives – women who have been steadfast in their love and attention, who have taken us under their wings and cared for us as one of their own. Less than six months after Suzy died, I attended a service for my "other" Mom.

Irene was a tour de force. Tall, beautiful, big-boned with high cheekbones suggesting her Slavic heritage, she had a warm, one hundred watt smile that could warm your soul. She was candid and no-nonsense in her motherly way.

I met Irene when I was about 14. She was a member of the cult I had joined. I'd often hitchhike to her home in Pine City, a few miles from Elmira. We drank coffee and smoked cigarettes and talked for hours.

When I was sent away to school, I saved my change and called her as often as I could. The calls continued regularly until she died – often once a week and sometimes more. Being a night owl, I rang her at odd hours, and I can only remember a few times when she didn't take my call. She was always there; always ready to listen to my thoughts and rants and dreams during long conversations. She was a rare and precious friend.

One day she left the group for her own reasons. She was an unusually private person and did not try to push me to leave, but respected where I was at the time.

Irene was ever-present and seemed nearly indestructible. She chain-smoked. She had a tumor, a monstrous teratoma the size of an orange, removed from her skull. Nonetheless, her memory was always sharp and clear – and much better than mine.

Very late in life, she fell in love for the first time with a man she had met. He became terminally ill and took his own life. She developed a serious heart problem. I called her and asked if what he had done had broken her heart, and she said yes. She passed away soon thereafter. Her loss was a keen and deep one.

Irene loved me like a son. I am sure I took those hundreds of calls for granted, never imagining that they could end.

Her family invited me to a service on the water. We scattered her ashes into Tampa Bay. To celebrate her life in this way was appropriate – that is what she wanted – but also important for closure and healing of those who survived her. Being a part of that helped to brook the transition from grief and sadness to acceptance and gratitude for the many years of great friendship.

Reflection: The notion that grief can be harmful – even fatal – stands out with Irene. Stories abound of spouses or lovers (seemingly in good health), who die soon after losing someone especially dear.

Instead, I have included Irene to highlight that as we age, our losses feel a bit like being at a shooting gallery: the shooter is relentless, and targets appear to fall at random, until there are none left standing.

Clay, my father's best friend, recently turned 100. He has three sons, along with several grandchildren and great-grandchildren. Clay has the mien, vitality, and cognition of a man in his 70s – you would never guess his true age. We keep in touch. He is the last living link to my father, and a gentle man.

Clay lost his wife several years ago, and he lived alone in their family home in Elmira. Suzy would visit him and fix him dinner and help him around the house. Eventually, a son in California suggested that he move west to join them, and he did.

I asked Clay if he expected to be happy to be with family again. It was really a rhetorical question, and his answer surprised me. He said that the most difficult thing about being so old was outliving all of your friends. His cohort was gone, and his family could not fill the void.

Irene's death underscored that loss is likely the most salient aspect of the game of life's fourth quarter. We know why, but the surprises of how and when await us.

Does the magnitude of grief lessen with each successive loss? Does it become "easier?" I don't know now, but I shall.

Coda

I've learned a lot. Some lessons have been hard.

Grief is really the other face of love; the tragedy mask that represents one-half of drama. We only mourn the things we cherish; if we did not care, we would not cry. It is also the unwelcomed, unbidden guest who suddenly appears on your doorstep. Sometimes there is advance warning; but it is just as apt to knock first by breaking down your door.

People grieve differently. There is no "one size fits all" when it comes to how people experience it, and so you have to be careful about making assumptions about other people's feelings and reactions, and where they are in the spectrum of grief.

There are no universally comforting words, and brevity is usually wise. Old-fashioned condolence notes are always appreciated and often cherished. A simple, paltry, "I'm so sorry" may suffice.

The best salve to someone grieving is just to be supportive company. Grief forces us to be present in the moment and for others.

I would be remiss not to mention how this past "Covid-19 fiscal year" has been an epic one for death, loss, and grief. The wounds of not being present with dying loved ones, or able to celebrate their lives at a decent funeral, will be with us long after the virus has faded. Many books will be written about the effects of the PTSD and unresolved losses that followed us into 2021 and beyond. Thankfully, that is not part of my own story or experience.

When I reflect upon my life's experience with loss, my reaction depended upon my situation in life, as well as my frame of mind. Grief changed from something that was always abhorrent to an instructor of what is truly important. I became mindful of a fundamental truth, that loss cannot be separated from life: everything that is or will become alive will perish. As we age, we will lose our parents, our friends – and eventually ourselves.

Yet it is not a zero-sum game: the love we extend while we are living endures, and ripples outward to eternity.

- Jonathan Yaeger
  June 2021

5 MITCH COHEN

A Jewish Man's Story

Grief Fail #1 - I Lose My Father, Part 1

It had just turned 1974. For months, I'd known my parents were separating. It made me feel ashamed and angry, and I buried it away deep inside, making believe it wasn't really going to happen. The year 1973 had been bad. My father was a victim of the major recession caused by the Arab Oil Embargo. Unfortunately, he chose that time to change careers, and the carpet store where he'd decided to try his hand at sales laid him off within months of hiring him.

**Engagement of Roz Bogen and Bob Cohen, circa 1952.
My mother was 19 and my father was 20.**

It wasn't his fault, but I couldn't shake my feeling of shame that he was out of work and couldn't find a job. None of my friends' fathers were out of work, so it seemed like it was just him. Of course, a 15-year-old can only see within the boundary of his house. The reality was many thousands were out of work. One thing, though, in my mind was clear. Unemployment may not have been his choice, but what was his choice — which ruined us financially — was the enormous debt he accrued borrowing from loan shark predators. Ultimately, this cost us our house in Englishtown, New Jersey and several years of pain and suffering to our family.

I was forced to share the financial humiliation. To pay bills, my parents took all my bar mitzvah money, which had been put away for my college education. My father even took the money I kept in my top dresser drawer, money I earned doing odd jobs in the neighborhood. He would leave IOU notes, which I suspected would never be paid back. I was right. They never were paid back.

During the winter of 1973, I walked door-to-door in the cold New Jersey wind, selling Christmas and holiday cards to earn points to win a bike. When I finished, I entrusted my father to mail in the collected money in return for the boxes of cards and a new 10-speed bike. After a month, I asked my mother when the cards and bike were going to arrive. She just looked at me and said that my father spent the money, and no cards or bike were going to arrive. One bright spot in my life during that dark period was that, a few months later, miraculously, the cards and the bike arrived! I don't know how he scraped up the money to send in, but he did. Or perhaps my mother paid for it, most likely with money borrowed from her sister or brother. I never asked and never knew. Like all the bad things that happened in our house, it never got discussed.

With my mother working full-time, I became the family cook, making dinner every night for us all. All we could afford were simple meals, and Hamburger Helper became a staple. We ate it at least three nights per week. To this day, I cannot eat Hamburger Helper and feel nauseous if I even glimpse a commercial for it.

By spring, it was my father's time to leave. My mother had thrown him out. One afternoon in April 1974, I simply heard the front door close. He didn't even say goodbye. I looked out of my window and saw him back out of the driveway in my grandfather's old red Rambler, which he had borrowed after the bank took away his car.

As my father backed the car into the street, shifted gears to drive and headed away, I felt my stomach drop. The reality I had been avoiding had come to pass. He was gone. I felt shocked. Anger, fear, and shame washed over me. I felt alone, not knowing what our life was going to be now. As I sat in shock at the end of my bed, my mother came in my room. She sat down next to me and started crying, "What am I going to do?" I was angry. She had no consoling, supportive words. She didn't even say, "what are we going to do," just "what am I going to do."

Me, age 17

I was a month shy of 16, and my adolescence had abruptly ended just after it had begun. I had to grow up fast and there was no training manual. Thus began 16 months of me struggling to serve as surrogate father to my younger brother and become the "man of the house."

While I didn't realize it at the time, grief had been in my life for some time, beginning with the financial stress and parental betrayal now capped off by my father leaving. At the time, I had no real knowledge of grief. I read about people grieving, thought it lasted a few days and was terrified of it. Like fear and sadness, I viewed grief as weakness.

Before he fell apart, my father had been the rock of the family. A brilliant guy, he could have been anything he wanted had he not been the son of a raging alcoholic who spent most of his life out of work or driving a taxi. My father grew up in the poor tenements of Williamsburg, Brooklyn, during the worst of the Great Depression. All he ever knew was failure, despair, and pain. Probably to help his own self-worth, he chose to be a savior to others who were suffering. This drew him to my mother when he was 17 and she was only 15 years young. She had lost her father to illness only two years earlier.

My mother was coddled by her two older siblings and became the type of self-centered person a coddled child often becomes. She always looked to others to take care of things for her. Thus, she was ill-equipped in 1974 to be abandoned by her "savior" husband. When my younger brother and I needed her most, she was wrapped up in her own world. My sister was 20 years old, out of school and working full-time.

For the first couple of weeks after my father left, I was numb. Filled with shame, I did not dare tell any of my friends what had happened. Always a sensitive kid, I felt defective and was vulnerable to the predators of the school yard. I wanted to be a tough guy but just didn't have it in me. I saw my sensitivity as a flaw and a part of me that had to be pushed down. In the working-class neighborhoods of Brooklyn and middle-class neighborhoods of central New Jersey where I grew up, male sensitivity was considered a weakness. I bought into this mindset early in my life.

I continued to bottle up my pain inside. About three weeks after my father left, my friends came over to hang out. Of course, I acted as if nothing was wrong, nothing had happened. Finally, my friend Kevin looked at me and said, "Mitch, we know that your father is gone. It's OK." I felt completely exposed, like I was caught in the spotlight of a prison guard while trying to escape. I was surprised at Kevin's compassion, something for which he was not known, but I didn't know how to respond. Continuing the pattern I'd learned from my parents, I quickly changed the topic and avoided discussion.

My grades at Manalapan High School started to fall, especially in biology, a class that I loved. When I quickly dropped from an A to a C, Mrs. Goldblatt called me out of class and into the hallway. She asked if anything was going on at home. I looked down tight-lipped, doing all I could to hold back the tears. As a high school tenth-grader, the last thing I wanted to do was to fall apart sobbing in the hallway. One teardrop did fall to the ground. I never spoke a word, and Ms. Goldblatt said nothing more. To this day, I have no idea if she called my mother. During this entire ordeal, my mother said nothing to me, never seemed to care how our father's failures and leaving affected me or my brother. It was always about her loss, her pain. I was left to deal with our family's losses alone, not knowing how to cope with any of it.

My father went to Atlanta where he eventually got his shit together. Still, I did not talk with him for almost six months, even though he called weekly. My mother started dating a nice guy. I was certain, even hopeful, that my parents would divorce, and we could all move on, even if that meant my father would never be with us again that was OK with me. I still had two uncles in Brooklyn who became father figures to me.

My anger at my father took over. Sadness became a daily visitor, especially when I started eleventh grade at a new high school, not knowing anyone. Food became my drug of choice to "stuff" the pain. I even binged and purged a few times though, fortunately, it did not turn into a habit.

Two things became my therapy: guitar and street hockey. I played guitar at least an hour each day, using two easy-chord Beatles books and listening to other band's records to learn their songs. I got a job at a nearby Italian restaurant as a dishwasher, saved up $100 and bought my first electric guitar and amp. The guitar would become a life-long passion.

My mother moved my brother and I to an apartment in Old Bridge, New Jersey. My old friends from Englishtown would come visit me, and a few came to play hockey on Sundays. I had made some friends at my new Madison Township High School, a few being street hockey players, and we formed a team with a few of my old friends from Englishtown. I was a dirty player. I think I relished releasing my repressed anger on our opponents in that parking lot rink at the East Brunswick Mall.

One weekend, my mother and her boyfriend went away on a trip. My brother was with a friend, and my sister had already left and moved down to Atlanta. At age 16, I was alone for the weekend, and it felt great.

Although I had not yet tried marijuana, I had started drinking beer on occasion with my friends back in Englishtown. As I kicked off my weekend alone in the small garden apartment in Old Bridge, I found a small bottle of Manischewitz kosher grape wine in the refrigerator and decided to have a glass. I listened to Pink Floyd's "Dark Side of the Moon," (1973) Paul McCartney's "Ram," (1971) and Emerson Lake & Palmer "Karn Evil Nine," (1973) back-to-back-to-back. A few hours later, I had consumed the entire bottle. I got sick soon after and had a horrible hangover the next day. However, I noticed that being drunk made the pain go away. Food no longer was my only means of avoiding pain.

By the fall of 1975, my parents reconciled and decided to move the rest of us to Atlanta. My father not only got his shit together; he got back his family. For my part, I gave him a second chance and got my father back after two years. That was the good news. The bad news was we never discussed what we had all been through, which for me was a lot. Between June 1974 and August 1975, I was forced to make two undesired moves; I attended three different high schools, including a new school in Atlanta for my senior year; I discovered marijuana; and I got kicked out of a high school dance for being intoxicated underage.

My mother continued to live in her own world and my father only looked forward, a wonderful trait, but not helpful for healing past wounds. Thus, unresolved grief made a home in my unconscious, only to be painfully released years later. Grief Fail #1 was complete.

Grief Fail #2 - First Real Death of a Loved One

My father's father, Max, who I called Grandpa, was a quiet man of few words. He met my grandmother, Paula, in 1928, just a few months after she arrived in the United States from Germany. Barely able to speak English, she worked at a diner in Brooklyn. My grandfather happened in and overheard some local guys teaching her English, except they were teaching her all bad words. They laughed as she looked back, bewildered.

Grandma Paula and Grandpa Max, circa 1961

Grandpa intervened and ran off the guys. Six weeks later, they were engaged. It was a whirlwind romance between a 17-year-old, poor Lutheran German woman, barely able to speak English, and the 19-year-old, poor Jewish son of Belarusian and Hungarian refugees. My great-grandparents refused to condone the wedding until my grandmother converted to Judaism. To be honest, I have no idea what Rabbi would have officiated a fast-track conversion, other than a Reform Jewish Rabbi. Apparently, that was acceptable to my strictly observant great-grandparents, and the young couple married shortly after her conversion.

While they were young, my grandfather and his sister spent some time in an orphanage after my great-grandfather suffered a back injury and my great-grandmother had an illness. I'm not sure how long they lived at the orphanage, but Grandpa and his sister were severely abused — physically, verbally, and emotionally — for the duration of their stay. They paid a dear price for the abuse. My grandfather developed a stutter, making him an easy target for bullies, and his sister ended up in a mental health hospital after a psychotic break. I never met her.

My grandfather became an alcoholic, probably to self-medicate and cope with the horrible circumstances he had faced. Back then, people just suffered from trauma and all the resulting collateral damage, without any possibility of mental health support or treatment, especially if they were poor. Fortunately, he beat his alcoholism after moving to Atlanta and at around age 64.

I loved Grandpa. He would sneak behind my grandmother and buy me the toy guns I wanted as a little boy. My grandmother was vehemently opposed to guns, having lost her father in France during World War I and a brother during World War II, both of whom fought for Germany.

For me, the hits just kept coming. I hadn't had nearly enough time to process the previous three years of family hell when, in 1977, just two years after we moved to Atlanta, my beloved Grandpa, a chain-smoking man who had worked as a plumber at the Brooklyn Navy Yard, developed a particularly vigorous and deadly type of lung cancer. I now suspect it was mesothelioma, which is asbestos-related cancer. He was 67 years old.

To help keep him busy, an uncle got Grandpa a job with a janitorial crew at the Atlanta IRS building. I also got a job there to be with him. Age 19, I teamed up with my grandfather for four hours, three evenings per week, stripping and waxing floors. Grandpa and I grew even closer.

Finally, when the cancer moved to his bones and the pain became unbearable, he stayed home, and doctors put him on morphine. Although given just weeks to live, he lasted about three months. I remember going over once to visit while he was in a morphine hallucination. He was yelling to my grandmother Paula, "Paulie, Get me outta here! Get me outta here!" I ran out of the house, jumped in my car, and, for the first time in years, fell apart and sobbed.

Even though this was a small release, emotions came flowing out uncontrollably. I beat the steering wheel in anger. Why is life so unfair? Why did our family have to go through so many horrible events in just four years? A lot of anger-related grief finally started trickling out. I quickly shut it down.

After my grandmother could no longer handle caring for him, Grandpa went back to the hospital. I refused to go see him. My father pushed me, and I went reluctantly, only to see him skin and bones and in a coma. I held his hand and said, "Grandpa, it's me." He squeezed my hand. When I told him that I had to go, he squeezed as hard as he could and would not let go. I pulled my hand away, ran out of the hospital and again lost it in my car.

Feeling alone and ashamed to cry in public, I used my car as my safe place to let out emotion. This would be a common safe place for me, especially years later when I suffered the biggest and most traumatic loss of my life.

On May 14, 1978, about two weeks after my last visit with him in the hospital, Grandpa passed away. Akin to the day my father left, I felt another punch in my stomach. My father coped by retreating to his room, lying in bed trying to sleep. Besides eating and smoking, sleeping was one of his favorite ways to avoid dealing with emotions.

At Grandpa's funeral, I did not cry. I refused to cry. One of my male cousins cried and I thought to myself, "He is a weakling; only the strong keep it together." As I would painfully learn later, nothing could have been further from the truth. After the funeral, we went back to my grandmother's house for a short, three-day period of mourning, and nobody cried. Grief Fail #2 was complete. My second major opportunity to learn a healthy way to grieve had passed.

During the mourning period, my father and uncles did what they always did — and what I had learned to do — use food and humor to cover pain. They also chain-smoked cigarettes. In my case, I used marijuana and alcohol. In fact, by 1978, I was smoking marijuana like a chimney, except during the week while I was studying engineering at Georgia Tech. Weekends were another matter. Weekends became blowout time for me. After a few years, the only thing that slowed me down was the fear of becoming an alcoholic like my grandfather and an uncle on my mother's side. That one fear likely saved me from addiction. However, food was still my drug of choice. It was so easy to stuff emotion with pizza – an entire half of a large pizza in one go. My pattern of not grieving continued. The sewer in my unconscious continued to fill, straining against the heavy, steel cap that was closed tightly shut; that is, until 2002.

Grief Fail #3 - I Lose My Father, Part 2 – This Time Forever

My mother and father, just three months before he died

It was the morning of May 20, 2002. My mother called sobbing, and I knew something bad had happened. It was a call I had feared for 15 years. "Something is wrong with Dad," she managed to gasp out. "I called the ambulance. You better meet us at the ER."

I dropped everything and headed down to St Joseph's ER. I ran inside and saw my brother doubled over crying. As I ran to him, I saw inside the curtained ER room. A doctor was literally on my father's chest doing CPR. I stood at his feet, watching this horrible scene. Figuring my father was dying, I chanted the Shema — the Jewish prayer that is to be the last prayer said by a dying person. One of the doctors must have been Jewish because he turned and looked me with horror in his eyes. This was hard for him, too. The English translation of what I chanted in Hebrew is, "Here O Israel, the Lord is God, the Lord is One."

Somehow my father pulled out of this total cardiac arrest. He seemed to be a master at defying death. He had survived a massive heart attack fifteen years earlier, getting zapped back to life twice in the ambulance, and colon cancer nine years earlier. Now he was being wheeled to ICU.

The doctor came in, looking shocked, and said he wasn't sure my father would pull through as his heart was now ninety percent damaged. Still, my father lived in a coma for three days before a neurologist ran an EEG and told us he was brain-dead. My mother, brother and sister all looked toward me for a decision. Other family members gathered. With my uncle, two aunts, and a few cousins also in the waiting room, I looked at everyone and made the call: we would take him off life support.

My sister, brother-in-law and I went in the room to be with my father as they removed the equipment keeping him alive. He struggled for air, as I imagine brain-dead people do as the body tries to survive. He looked like a little baby sucking for air. It hurt to watch.

He finally stopped struggling and breathed one last breath. He was gone. Grief, Part Two, Dad is Gone for Good, had begun. All the unresolved grief of my parental 18-month separation was released from the sewer of my unconscious, to be added to the grief of my father's death. Overwhelmed is putting it lightly. Somehow, I held it together for his funeral. I even delivered his eulogy, which I did not think was possible. I had learned to hide my emotions and be strong from my father. Yet I did not learn how to process his death or his life. These patterns unfortunately are learned patterns when we are children, and I was repeating what I had observed. However, my father also showed us what resilience looks like, his deep passion for music and his great sense of humor, which were gifts for which I will always be grateful.

I sat at my parent's house for the requisite Jewish seven-day period of deep mourning. It was during this time that I reflected on my father's successes in life and not only his one big failure. In fact, when delivering his eulogy, I mentioned that he taught me that from the depths of failure, one can learn from mistakes, rise up, reinvent oneself and succeed at life. He did that and deserved the credit I offered up about him. At the end of the seven days, I suggested that we walk around the community, to ritualize the cycle of life and our need to begin walking forward. Grief Fail #3 was complete, except I was about to get a major lesson about how failing to grieve can manifest itself in the body.

I went back to work, incorrectly thinking that my grief period was over. That's when the panic attacks and palpitations started, along with a consistent heart rate of about 100, which I had never experienced. Because I was a runner, my heart rate was typically in the low 60s. I was scared. Eighteen years of unresolved grief, along with the current grief, was making its way out of my mind via my body in quite a scary and painful way.

Depression, though not altogether foreign to me, had not really been an issue for almost 10 years. I experienced my first "visit" of mild depression after I graduated from Georgia Tech. Now, it came roaring back. I wasn't sleeping or eating well. I obsessed over my heart palpitations, which only made them worse. One night, I was out of town for a training class and woke up at three in the morning, gripped in one of the scariest panic attacks that I ever had. I had no idea what was happening or what to do. I went into the bathroom of the dormitory where I was staying, hoping someone would come in so I could beg them to walk with me across the street to the nearby University hospital. I was convinced that I was dying.

It took almost two months for my heart rate to come down from in the high 90s to normal. Yet another month passed before the panic attacks finally waned. The last one came unexpectedly while I was watching a hockey game on TV. This time, I somehow knew to just breathe into it. Miraculously, it subsided, I was OK, and I never had a panic attack again. I learned firsthand that unresolved and unprocessed grief festers in the mind and body. Eventually, it will find its way out, beating the living shit out of you on the way.

#4 Finally grieving for real: The loss of my wife to suicide.

Suzette on our wedding day, September 4, 1983

Suzette had struggled ever since being fired from the Marcus Atlanta Jewish Community Center, a result of her simply ending up on the wrong side of workplace politics. Being progressive Jews, Suzette and I had often bumped heads with the Director. Her performance appraisals had always been great, but the program she helped manage was disliked by the Adult Education Director. I don't solely blame Suzette's ensuing depression on that firing; however, it did trigger a deeply buried sense of worthlessness and failure that she had repressed all her life.

Suzette was brilliant. Blessed with a photographic memory, she breezed through college, but she always held back from challenging herself and tended to play small. When motherhood arrived with our firstborn son, she finally played big. In becoming a mother, she not only found an identity — she became that identity. Being a mother to our three sons was who Suzette was. Wrapping her self-worth so tightly around being the mother of our sons proved to be a second trigger of her depression at age 52.

On top of losing her job, one of our sons and his girlfriend were planning their wedding. I believe Suzette viewed the marriage of any one of our sons as a huge threat to her persona and whole identity as Mother – the boys had grown up into men. She seemed unable to face the fact that all three of our sons would eventually marry and leave the nest.

2010, Vermont at the Ben & Jerry's factory

Then there was a third trigger. Underneath all these life circumstances, locked up deep in her own inner basement, was a latent bipolar gene that she inherited from her father, a Holocaust survivor, who suffered greatly from what was thought to be post-traumatic stress disorder. In hindsight, we believe he had bipolar disorder. The gene expressed itself in Suzette as she entered menopause and dealt with her firing and our son's marriage.

Suzette finally agreed to see a psychotherapist, and her family doctor prescribed Ambien and Paxil. Nothing seemed to work until our consulting functional medicine doctor checked her hormone levels and found they were out of whack. Menopause was really kicking in, and it diminished her hormones, especially progesterone. The doctor prescribed a bioidentical hormonal medication and within four days of starting the medicine, Suzette was back! It was like a miracle.

Jordan, Eric and Zachary – circa 1991. Suzette loved them without bounds and lived for them without question.

The miracle lasted almost 18 months, but it came with a price. She was very happy, a little too happy, and she became a bit aggressive. She wanted to upgrade our home flooring and build a deck. She became somewhat impulsive, the life of the party. In retrospect, we believe she was mildly manic; it was not a huge upswing, but still manic.

We had urged her to see a psychiatrist, but she didn't want to do so. After 18 months of experiencing the "miracle" recovery, at my urging and the non-psychiatrist doctor's urging, she began to ween off the Paxil. We all hoped that her insights during the 18 months of therapy would give her back her life. About 45 days later, however, she started the second downturn. The miracle was over.

This time, after about two months of anxiety and depression, she got back on an earlier regimen that seemed to help: Ambien and Paxil. We had her hormones retested, and she got on a new prescription of bioidentical hormones. I still don't know if she had stopped taking them during the miracle period.

The fourth day of the new bioidentical hormone treatment began on the morning of January 12, 2013. We were waiting for another miracle. The last time she had started hormones, it was the fourth day that the miracle happened. But this time, on this fourth day, Suzette woke up feeling terrible. I told her to give it another couple of days and if it didn't kick in, we would go back to the functional medicine doctor. She still did not want to see a psychiatrist; I believe it was a shame issue for her.

I was training to be a yoga instructor and had a class to go to that morning. With Suzette feeling so bad, I was ambivalent about going, but I also felt I needed a caretaker break. I promised her, "When I get back, we will go to the DeKalb Farmers Market." This was something she loved. I stepped outside that unusually warm, winter Saturday and hesitated again outside the door. Should I stay or should I go?

I chose to go to yoga. When I arrived home after class, the van was in the driveway, so I knew she was home. I called her name but there was no answer. "She's probably sleeping," I thought.

I climbed the stairs, continuing to call her name. I walked into our bedroom and saw she wasn't in bed. Then I turned and looked to my right. While I was gone, she had hanged herself from the door to the master bathroom.

Not believing what I was seeing, I looked and then saw the bungie cord. I screamed, "NO!!!!!!!!!!!!!!, NO!!!!!!!!!!!!!!!" I ran over and pulled her off the cord, but it was too late. The look of death in a human's face with open eyes speaks volumes. She was gone.

I sat on the bed, sobbing, and breathing heavily. I called 9-1-1 and they had me stay on the phone with them as I described what had happened in between short breaths. I heard a faint siren in the distance approaching and yelled into the phone, "NO SIRENS!!!!!!!!" The siren stopped.

After the Firefighters arrived and confirmed Suzette's death, they told me to go downstairs and sit in the living room. I wanted to stay upstairs, but they would not let me. It dawned on me that my home was now a crime scene, and I was considered a murder suspect.

After about 45 minutes, they brought down her body. They said they were sorry. They said the coroner would contact me with details, advising that an autopsy would be done as is customary when foul play is a possibility. Fortunately, the coroner's office expedited the autopsy and performed it the next day.

Once they were gone, I was faced with the hardest task of my life. I called our boys. Even in my horrible shock, I knew I had to call them, and I did. That was the hardest thing that I've ever had to do. They all knew that Suzette was suffering but did not know the extent; none of us knew. Like too many people who suicide out of life, Suzette kept to herself the profoundness of her pain.

Our family, just 7 months before Suzette died

Two days later, more than 700 people paid their respects at Suzette's funeral, which we held on January 14 because January 15 was her birthday. Later I learned that many people suicide near birthdays, anniversaries, or holidays.

I delivered the eulogy. As when my father died, some sort of survival gear inside me kicked in, helping me do what seemed impossible. In keeping with Jewish custom, the service concluded as friends and family shoveled soil onto Suzette's casket until it was covered. After everyone had gone, I stayed behind and asked the backhoe operator if I could fill her grave with the remaining soil.

Kindly, and in violation of every possible safety code, they showed me how to operate the backhoe, and I filled the rest of her grave myself. I wanted no stranger to fill it.

For the first time in my life, I decided to write in a journal. I finally accepted that grief takes time and works on its schedule, so being open to whatever came up and writing it down seemed like a good way to process. In the early days after her death, I remained in shock and disbelief. I felt like a little boy, abandoned and alone. For almost six weeks, I lived in turn with my sister-in-law and then with my mother-in-law. When I finally went back to our house, two of my sons took turns living with me for another two months. I needed to be around people all the time. When I was alone, the pain was too intense. For the first time in my life, I could not stuff down the pain. With the loss of Suzette, the years of repressed grief were being fully flushed out of the basement sewer, and I could barely function.

I wasn't sleeping or eating. I decided to go to a psychiatrist who prescribed a low dose of Zoloft to fend off the worst of the depression I anticipated. As I've mentioned before, I was no stranger to depression. Almost annually, in the fall because of past trauma, I was visited by anxiety and mild depression. (Fortunately, eventually I addressed this in therapy.) It was my choice to be on a low dose, just 25 mg of Zoloft, which the doctor advised might as well be a placebo, but I was OK with that. I didn't want to completely numb out the pain. I just wanted to keep the bottom from falling out. At night, I also took a low dose of Seroquel, a mood stabilizer, to help mitigate the side effects of Zoloft and to promote REM sleep. Never a fan of medication, I took whatever the psychiatrist prescribed. I weaned off the Seroquel after six months.

After about a week, the initial shock of Suzette's death wore off, then the anger kicked in. I was angry about everything and at everyone.

I was angrier with no one more than Suzette. One journal entry says, "I feel angry that you left me; I feel angry that you left the boys, I feel angry that I am alone; I feel angry that you just couldn't wait for me to get home from yoga and talk; I feel angry that our lives are upside down – all of us!"

I was angry with the maker of Ambien, which she had been taking to help her sleep. I was convinced she went into a hallucination and took her life unknowingly. For a while I wanted to sue the company. I went so far as to talk with an attorney.

As is common with suicide loss, I was overwhelmed with guilt and questioning why. At the same time, I was consumed with anger. I went over everything said or not said for the two to three weeks before Suzette's death. I looked for hints that I had missed. I tore the house apart looking for a suicide note, only not to find one.

I focused on one short conversation we had the night before her death. She asked me, "Why do you stay with me?" I thought for several seconds, wanting to say, "Because who else would have me?" In retrospect, I wish I had replied, "Because I love you, even when you feel bad." However, in a "Fiddler on the Roof" (1964) moment, all I said was, "Well, why wouldn't I stay with you?"

The guilt about this short conversation wrapped me in knots for weeks. Did I push her over the edge? What did I miss? What could I have done? I felt horribly guilty about the times I fantasized about running away to California, away from all my resentments and regrets. I came to find out that this is typical for those who lose loved ones to suicide. It is common to feel tremendous guilt about what was said or not said, what was done or not done. It was an excruciating feeling, thinking that I could have been responsible for her suicide.

Another entry in my journal: "I really, really, really miss you. I feel ripped off, lost, without knowing what to do. There is a huge hole in our hearts – how could you do this to us?"

I never slept in our bedroom again, not once after January 12, 2013, not even when my sons and their partners stayed with me. I barely ever went in that room again. I moved clothes into my younger sons' shared bedroom and slept in a twin bed for a year. I kept our master bedroom door closed. My world became my sons' bedroom and their small bathroom.

Three weeks after Suzette's funeral, I realized I needed grief therapy. I called The Link Counseling Center in Sandy Springs, Georgia, which specializes in aftercare for the survivors who have lost loved ones to suicide. Whether it was an act of grace or mere serendipity, the Director of Counseling, who did all initial intakes, had a rare opening that day and I jumped on it. He proved to be the exact lifeline and therapist that I needed. We met weekly for two years, and I continued to see him regularly for the next seven years.

I placed a large photograph of Suzette by the twin bed and yelled at it every day. I screamed at the top of my lungs. I beat the hell out of pillows and punched the bed. Every night for a couple of weeks, I went outside and yelled at God, "How did you let this happen? She was a wonderful mother, wife, teacher, social worker! You stopped Abraham from killing Isaac, why didn't you stop her?" My neighbors must have thought I was going crazy. If they did, they were right.

I couldn't go back to the yoga studio for almost two months. In my mind, it was going there that prevented me from saving Suzette. Instead, I did my own yoga practice at home. Every morning after my yoga practice, I would lie on the mat and cry. For three solid months I cried daily on my yoga mat.

I threw every possible therapy and treatment at my grief. I saw an acupuncturist and an energy healer weekly for about three months. I even met a Shaman. I sought support whenever and wherever I could get it, in any way, shape, or form. Close friends became my sounding board. My oldest son's father-in-law became a trusted friend. He even took me to see a PTSD therapist; however, for some good reason, I never experienced PTSD responses to Suzette's death and discovering her body. Being open to alternative healing and seeking nontraditional healers were not a stretch for me and proved to be very helpful.

Because of all my past, unresolved grief, which had been compounded by Suzette's death, I chose to spend 20-30 minutes in bed upon waking every morning simply lying there and feeling whatever came up, without judgment or resistance. At times, the pain I felt was overwhelming; sometimes my body shook and shuddered, yet I knew this was an important part of my grief work. I was paying the price for avoiding past grief.

After these morning "unload" sessions in bed, I often journaled what had come up that day. One morning, I sobbed in bed, yelling out, "I want my mommy! I want my mommy!" I knew that many soldiers wounded in the field often call out for their mothers. This looking for maternal nurturing is a primal, infant-like response to pain. I was a 54-year-old man calling out for his mommy. Though surprised, I somehow knew it was just part of the process. I brought this to therapy. To my surprise, my therapist seemed almost excited that I had experienced such a primal response. For the first and only time, I thought he was the one who was nuts!

After two months of this daily morning "check in" with my suffering, I still felt angry, lonely, and abandoned. At times, I felt I was trapped in a hole and would never find my way out, but I continued the daily work and weekly therapy.

One spring day, about four months after Suzette's death, I was outside in the backyard, and it started to rain. A thunderstorm was fast approaching, and the lightning was getting closer. I looked up at the dark clouds bearing down on me and yelled. "OK, you motherfucker – here is your chance – go ahead and strike me dead! Go ahead you son of a bitch – I dare you, you bastard!"

I was struck that day, but not by lightning. Instead, I had an epiphany that marked a turning point in my grief. First, I fired God and Judaism for the second time in my life. (The first time was at age 15, and it had taken me another 15 years to rediscover both.) I realized that God did not cause Suzette's depression and could not have prevented her death. Rather, biology caused her depression and an uncontrollable need to stop her pain caused her death. I let God off the hook. It wasn't God's fault.

Second, I realized that God had no control over anything bad, painful, or horrific that had ever happened to me, or anyone. I fired the God that organized religion had forced upon me. I began to look for the God within all creation – good and bad. In the months ahead, I also discovered the Divine within the human heart, as so many reached out to support me and provide rich listening. For me, there no longer was a God out there – there was only the Divine within all of us and all of creation. "Namaste" was a correct greeting.

Soon thereafter, the husband of a Rabbi acquaintance asked me to be in a book study group with him. He felt that I would be open to the book he wanted to study. It was another experience of serendipity. The book was titled *Everything is God: The Radical Path of NonDual Judaism,* by Jay Michaelson (2009). The study group never happened, and the book sat unread on my other son's bed in the room for several weeks.

I had concluded that God didn't stop Suzette from killing herself because God isn't out there with any control of anything, but one day I picked up the book and began reading. It changed my entire approach to Judaism, theology, and spirituality. Buddhist psychology became a source of study. Grief had broken me open, and I surrendered to it. My own archetypal personal suffering, inner death, and transformation had begun.

"There's a crack, a crack in everything;
That's how the Light gets in"
-Leonard Cohen, "Anthem" (1992)

I also started working with Anne Brener's book, *Mourning and Mitzvah* (2001), a kabbalistic walk through the entire first year of Jewish ritual mourning until the unveiling of the tombstone. It is a great book, with discussion, journal exercises and guidance along all the milestones through a year-long grief journey. Of course, no grief journey magically ends at year one, but it metaphorically symbolizes getting back into life after a year. I highly recommend this book, regardless of one's religion.

About three and a half months after Suzette's death, I began talking more often with a female friend, Stella, whose name I have changed to protect her privacy. Stella was going through a divorce. I always had many female friends with whom I could talk about real things. During my marriage to Suzette, I even had a lesbian friend who I called my "safe girlfriend," because we grew very close without the sexual attraction.

Suzette and I had known Stella and her husband well for about four years. Stella was a former student of mine as well as Suzette, but she spent more time learning with Suzette. Stella was a Jew by choice and Suzette taught her about how to raise Jewish children. Stella loved Suzette and was grieving for her, too.

Stella and I met for lunch and talked on the phone about what we were both going through. I started to have strong feelings for Stella and talked with my therapist about this. He told me that attraction in the months after the loss of a spouse was not uncommon, as it was usually a sign of missing the connection and intimacy of the lost spouse.

My therapist did not discourage me yet told me to watch out. He said that we needed to make sure that I wasn't short-circuiting grief if the relationship with Stella progressed beyond friendship. I promised to keep him informed of what was happening with my grieving process and with my friendship with Stella.

By June, almost six months after Suzette's death, my relationship with Stella did develop into a romantic relationship. I discussed this at great length with my therapist, not wanting to be one of those men who avoided grief and jumped into something new. However, my fear and loneliness got the better of me.

In Stella's defense, she loved Suzette and was also grieving her loss. In the first year of our relationship, she did give me space to grieve, to talk about Suzette and we both comforted each other in our grief, she for her marriage, and me for my wife. My therapist reminded me of the 90 percent failure rate of relationships that occur soon after divorce or death. Sadly, this proved to be true for Stella and myself. We should have remained friends. After we both had mostly recovered from our losses, our personality differences started to create lots of conflict – especially during arguments, which were frequent. The relationship ended after three years. I learned a lot from our time together and we remain friendly. We both supported each other through difficult times.

In retrospect, I have no major regrets about my relationship with Stella, as I still worked through my grief the entire time. She never discouraged me or tried to shut me down, which is often what happens during a relationship formed soon after a major loss, so I was lucky in that respect. Nonetheless, even with good memories of my time with Stella, I wish I had learned to live with the fear and loneliness while I processed my grief. This might have allowed me to fully focus on processing the grief and go through it fully engaged and not distracted by a relationship.

Five and a half years after Suzette's death, I did meet a wonderful woman with whom I have now built a meaningful and loving life. As a small girl, she lost her mother to suicide, so she has some understanding of what I had been through.

After a year of weekly therapy at The Link, I joined a monthly "Survivors of Suicide" (SoS) peer support group at The Link. Some join an SoS Group early on in their grief, but it took me a year before I was ready for group work. A year or so after that, I trained at The Link to facilitate groups and started a new SoS Group in Decatur, Georgia, near where I lived. I wanted to support others new to the tough and complicated journey of grief after the loss of a loved one to suicide. I wanted to draw from my experiences – both the mistakes and what worked – with others. As it was a peer group, I also got to share my process, which supported my ongoing work of recovery.

Lessons I Learned

Until Suzette's death and my subsequent, long grief journey, I couldn't be comfortable with my sensitivity or my feelings. From an early age, I learned to fear grief. When I experienced anger, shame, sadness, or shock, rather than taking the time to process those emotions and grieve, I learned to stuff those feelings away, first using food and later alcohol and drugs.

As mentioned earlier, my first extended "visit" from mild depression came when I was 23 and just graduated from college. It lasted almost two months and began what I describe as an awakening experience over an entire year. While the cracks started to open my armor, a lot more opening remained to do. I needed to feel a lot less shame about letting out those feelings.

By pushing down my feelings to the "basement" of my psyche, a volcanic eruption of grief built up. It would take years and another trauma, the death of my father, to lift the sewer cover to slightly off the storage tank. However, this release of grief expressed itself through bodily sensations and physiology, rather than emotion. By the time Suzette died, there was no turning away raw emotional grief any longer. The sewer cap flew off, and the ensuing hard, painful work of processing, grieving, and healing from this long-overdue release of emotions consumed me for almost three years.

The loss of my wife was the catalyst that finally drove me to deal with years of stored-away grief. With the help of my grief counselor, well-schooled in Jungian Depth Psychology; a support group at The Link Counseling Center; and the low dose of Zoloft, to help me get through but avoid numbing out the pain, I gradually worked my way through my journey, grieving each loss of my life so many years later.

What I finally learned is that vulnerability is my superpower. Being vulnerable and sharing what I was experiencing in the presence of loving and caring friends, family and my therapist was the only way through.

Going deep inside and working to befriend and unburden young, wounded parts of my sub-personality allowed those wounded parts to let go, release pain, and start to heal. My healing grief journey started later in life, at age 54. But no matter one's age, I believe it is never too late to grieve.

The only bad grief is not grieving.

On August 4, 2018, I met Hannah. After five and one-half years of grieving, I found a life partner and new love with whom I will spend the rest of my life.

As this book is about to go to print, I must add one more painful sharing about grief. On May 15, 2023, Garcia, my beloved Golden Retriever of 13 ½ years died. His health had been declining for months, and I knew the time was coming; however, I didn't want to decide to euthanize him too soon, or too late. Over the past year, he lost vision in his left eye and his back legs became wobbly. He kept trucking along. I cannot remember the last time he sat down, because he could not get up from a sitting position. He would just lay down and then pull himself up with his front legs, which most of the time worked. Other times, we lifted him up.

Monday, May 15, started as a good day. A home groomer came for the first time, and she did a fantastic job. Garcia felt good – he rolled around on the front lawn, though I had to help him get up. After dinner, I took him for his normal 7:30 PM walk and he did his business. When we got home, he drank water and laid down on the carpet near his water bowl, which he often did in the evening. I looked down and noticed something odd.

His left front leg began to tremble, which had never happened before. Then his mouth started to open and close with a tremble. Within seconds, his entire body was in full massive seizure. It was horrible to witness. He was running in place and bouncing on the floor. When he began to foam at the mouth, we knew he had to be rushed to the pet hospital.

My love Hannah, her son and her son's fiancé jumped into action, as I could not lift him up. They both ran and got a sheet, carried him to the back of my car and we headed toward the pet hospital. I knew it was time.

As we left the development where we live, I burst into tears and said, "we have to put him down. He cannot go through this again". We got to the Blue Pearl Animal Hospital, who had treated Garcia back in 2017, and they rushed out to take him in. Once they stabilized the convulsions, we all sat in a consultation room.

Dr. Baker, the wonderful doctor, who was so compassionate and kind, explained what was going to happen. We sat with Garcia, hands on him, me crying and letting him know that he will always be my boy, tried to get in front of his face, so he could see me. I always wanted to be the last thing he saw and I'm not sure my wish came true. I may not have gotten close to his good right eye. At least he could hear me.

Dr. Baker injected the medicine and declared Garcia gone. I broke down hysterically. The pain of losing Garcia was intense. He was more than a dog for me; he was my service dog. He was at my wife's feet when she died. He was with me during the first horrible year of grief for my wife. He was there when two relationships ended, one in 2017 and one short relationship in 2018. He was always there. When I was on my own and lonely, he sat with me. It was the two of us.

For the next two weeks after his death, I went out each day, at the scheduled time and "walked" him. I talked with him, just as I had, encouraging him to pee or poop. I burst into tears each time. I'm still engaged in the same ritual, though only once per day, and I don't know how long it will take before I stop "walking" him. I don't know how long it will take to grieve his loss and it's OK. Grief works on its time, not ours.

It took me most of my life to allow myself to be vulnerable, and I will not short-circuit any part of the grief process. Just because I've learned a thing or two about grief, does not exempt me from loss or experiencing the needed grief after loss. I've come to accept that I am a sensitive human being, who feels deeply. I love deeply, I laugh heartily, and I cry intensely when sad. Maybe it's just part of the aging process or perhaps all the psychotherapy I've done myself, reinforced by the grief counseling that I do with my clients.

Grief is part of the human condition. Being vulnerable, embracing the unknown and openly expressing emotion, regardless of any fears about how others will perceive me is the only way through.

"If I knew the way, I would take you home" - Jerry Garcia, for whom Garcia was named.

"Go home now Garcia"
- Phil Foster, a fellow spiritual journeyman and my friend

6 A THERAPIST'S PERSPECTIVE

Grief - an Internal Family Systems (IFS) Therapist's Perspective

The challenges of grief often lead the bereaved to seek psychological and spiritual counseling among the many varied branches or schools of psychological and spiritual practice. For example, Jungians might have a different approach from Gestalt Psychology or Behaviorism, but all would aspire to reduce patient suffering and promote healing.

This final chapter will draw from an important work by Derek Scott, a licensed Certified IFS therapist, founder of the Internal Family Systems Counseling Association (IFSCA) and master teacher of IFS. Derek teaches IFS all over the world and has supported hundreds of therapists, coaches and spiritual directors through his course, "Stepping Stone," an intensive 16-week course.

For a complete version of the document from which this chapter was derived, Self-Led Grieving: Transitions, Loss & Death, reach out to the IFSCA at www.ifsca.ca.

I selected this school of thought because it is one that I am most familiar with:

"Internal Family Systems (IFS) is an approach to psychotherapy that identifies and addresses multiple sub-personalities or families within each person's mental system. These sub-personalities consist of wounded parts and painful emotions such as anger and shame, and parts that try to control and protect the person from the pain of the wounded parts. The sub-personalities are often in conflict with each other and with one's core Self, a concept that describes the curious, confident, compassionate, whole person that is at the core of every individual. IFS focuses on healing the wounded parts and restoring mental balance and harmony by changing the dynamics that create discord among the sub-personalities and the Self." *Psychology Today, https://www.psychologytoday.com/us/therapy-types/internal-family-systems-therapy)*

The IFS model was created in the 1980s by Psychologist, Richard (Dick) C. Schwartz. The model grew out of the work Schwartz did as a family therapist. He noticed certain dynamics going on within families that could also apply to his individual clients' inner worlds. His theory came into play when working with individuals with eating disorders, where a client would say, "Part of me had to eat the entire gallon of ice cream and then another part shamed me horribly for eating it." Schwartz started to work with the client's inner family, as parts consisting of Protectors and Exiles as he worked with client's external family of parents and children in family counseling sessions. Dick Schwartz went on to found the Internal Family Systems Institute and has written a number of great books.

As a practitioner of the model on IFS, grief counselors, life coaches and therapists draw from the inner world parts approach to grief.

To understand the parts model, all of us have been asked from time to time and responded similarly:

Partner or friend, "where would you like to go tonight?"

Us, "Part of me wants to go to the movies and part of me just wants to stay home,"

Or

Partner or friend, "what movie would you like to see?"

Us, "Part of me wants to see 'Respect' and part of me wants to see 'James Bond'."

These inner conversations are going on all the time inside our minds and these are examples of how we speak them externally. Perhaps you can see that we all have inner worlds with these parts, so let's relate this parts model to grief work. First, a brief introduction is needed.

In the IFS model, all of us have an inner family of personality parts, similar to our external families. Externally, we have parents, siblings, friends and perhaps children. Inside us, we have a similar family; however, these are parts of our inner world. The model asserts that we all have protective parts, like inner parents that work hard to minimize further pain to young, vulnerable child-like inner parts, hurt so long ago. The Protectors can be Managers, who are proactive, scanning the horizon to avoid people, situations or experiences that might trigger a younger, vulnerable, wounded part of our inner world. Protectors can also be Firefighters, who are reactive – once a younger, vulnerable, wounded part is activated or triggered, the Firefighter does all it can to distract, repress or "put out the fire." Some refer to Firefighters as First Responders, as they are both reactive and rush to protect triggered wounded, younger parts of the psyche.

The younger, vulnerable, wounded parts are like children inside, who to protect them from further harm, were exiled deep within. In Jungian psychology, this would be exiled to the shadow – that which we avoid. However, Exiles are stuck back in time, typically the age of the first injury. Protectors are also stuck back in time when they took on the extreme job of protecting the wounded exile. The Restoration Cluster is the group of neo-Exiles still holding the pain of grief and Managers looking ahead for ways to live without whom or what was lost. Typically, the neo-Exiles might still be holding the pain of loss, yet not as intensely as directly after the loss. Therefore, the Restoration Cluster is the tension between parts feeling the pain of grief and parts starting to move forward.

Please note that in IFS, some refer to the group of inner parts as "the system." In other words, the system is made up of Protectors (Managers, Firefighters and Exiles). Others refer to the system as the psyche. Both are interchangeable.

A caveat is necessary here. Parts work of any sort, which was also called Inner Child work is **NEVER** about blaming our parents, siblings, extended family members, friends, etc. While some of them did or said some shaming and hyper-critical things, it is still our job to do our own inner work to unburden the wounded Exiles and give the Protectors a break from their hard work.

There is an energy inside all of us that is not a part of our personality, our inner family. Jung and many others referred to this energy as Self. For those with a spiritual understanding of Self, this would be one's True Nature, Core Essence, Inner Divine, etc.

All of us also have Self-energy. People who meditate, engage in contemplative prayer or other practices and get to that totally relaxed, oneness state are fully accessing Self-energy. People with hobbies can recall getting lost in time, deep diving into their passion – that is Self-energy.

The work of IFS is to develop an ability to be led by Self-energy. The therapist, coach or grief counselor guides the client with many open-ended questions, so that the client can access their own Self-energy to unburden their own parts.

We know we have accessed our Self-energy when we are experiencing:

- Compassion
- Curiosity (with no judgment)
- Centeredness
- Courage to explore
- Clear mindedness
- Creativity
- Confidence
- Calmness

If there are emotion and sensations present, then a part has blended, or joined with Self-energy. Think of Protectors and Exiles as being clouds and Self-energy as the Sun (the Light within). When too many clouds are present, blocking the Sun, then Self-energy cannot come forth.

If there is no emotion and just a deep sense of curiosity, appreciation and compassion for what the Protectors do and what the Exiles feel, then we are in Self-energy.

By holding our Self-energy, we can learn about the jobs of our protective parts of our personality, get clear on why they work so hard and what they fear would happen if they didn't work so hard. Being in our Self-energy also provides the safe space for our young, vulnerable and hurt parts of our personality to come out of hiding. Once they feel safe, they will open up and share their pain, looking to witness and eventually release it and heal. Only then will the Protectors step back some and work less hard.

Our goal in IFS part work is for the client – all of us – to learn to be Self-led in healing our own wounded young parts and gaining the trust of our Protectors to let us from Self-energy lead the entire inner world of our personality.

Self-Led Grieving: Transitions, Loss and Death
By Derek Scott, Founder of IFSCA and Registered Social Worker

Loss is not a problem to be solved. It's an unavoidable recurring life event to which we adapt by grieving. Although grief never feels simple, simple grief is differentiated as grief that runs its natural course without obstacle, from grief that is made complicated either by unresolved prior loss or by the traumatic nature of the loss. When grief is simple and straightforward, the job of the therapist is to be a companion and occasional guide for the bereaved client, keeping company and embodying the therapist's own Self-energy, a state of mind characterized by presence, curiosity and compassion. However, when the bereaved isolates and feels overwhelmed or bewildered by loss, it is likely that the parts of their inner system are holding stories of unsupported loss in the past, which means more Complicated Grief has arisen and the work is for our therapist or support team to hold space, to hear the stories and help the parts to release years of held pain and to heal.

Common complications that arise in grieving people, include their non-acceptance, guilt, shame, isolation, problematic (or absent) social supports, depression and possible suicide ideations. Grief can be complicated by unresolved early or traumatic loss, which can show up in the delay, absence or chronicity of grief.

Many therapists have heard clients new to therapy say things like, "my family was good, they never beat me or anything." Clients can have protective parts summarize childhood as not too bad or pretty good on the whole. While Protectors can gloss over adversity and report no significant early losses and may be casual as they mention the death of a beloved one, they may block other parts who have helpful information about the client's distress and ways of coping.

The therapist can combine a classic bereavement tool with IFS by taking a loss history. The loss history gives the client an opportunity to acknowledge his losses, notice how he survived and appreciate his resilience. At the same time, his history may give the therapist insight into his current response to loss. In order to be as complete as possible with this history, it is good to know what support was at the time, what the client was told about loss and what his parts learned from watching the way others responded to loss.

Loss is inherent to the many transitions of childhood. When parents separate, for example, a child may lose the future he expected along with his current life. When a family pet dies, a child may have lost a virtual sibling or a magical being who held many confidences. When a family moves to a new house, a child may lose the fabric and structure of her world. When the therapist and support team listen with open hearted curiosity, they hear about the client's attachments and the significance of his losses, which may not be what we would have assumed.

The journey of grief can be described as three phases of parts of our inner personality needing lots of attention: (1) the First Responder parts, (2) the Grief Cluster of parts, and (3) the Restoration Cluster of parts. The First Responders are Firefighters, who react to loss with shock, disbelief, denial and numbness, are often closely paired with story-telling parts. They titrate the influence of our more vulnerable, wounded Exile parts (who will only be revealed gradually) and allow Managers to cope with required practicalities like arranging funeral services. It takes time for the therapist and support team to hold space for the First Responder parts to share and tell their stories. This is not a time for "advice giving" or offering platitudes – it is a time for deep listening for our own Self-energy, staying present, curious and compassionate.

Since grieving can't be rushed, many sessions or conversations of sharing and witnessing may be needed. Periods of deep sadness and strong emotion will bring on fatigue, scatteredness and forgetfulness. The opposite of depression is not happiness, but "vitality". Since vitality is usually absent for a time during bereavement, the bereaved may wonder if he was feeling depressed. But, answering his question at that moment would have taken him out of grieving. When the deep sadness and reality of the loss begins to sink in, the bereaved is experiencing the Grief Cluster of parts.

The Grief Cluster is the recent group of sad and traumatized Exiles of the psyche who are protesting, missing, searching, longing, regretting and feeling guilty about the current loss. These parts help us on the unavoidable journey after we lose what we need and love. Whether or not they are connected to earlier unresolved losses, Grief Cluster Exiles are generally held at a distance until Protectors are convinced that the system can tolerate their distress without being overwhelmed.

Unlike the young, vulnerable wounded inner parts kept in hiding as Exiles from our outer world for many years, the Grief Cluster of parts may not have been held in exile for years or for that long. Unlike Exiles connected to childhood events whose stories are kept out of awareness until a person's Self-energy is available, Grief Cluster parts are often "Neo-Exiles," or new Exiles wounded by the current loss, held in abeyance at first, so that their experiences can be heard, held and assimilated gradually.

Knowing this both normalizes and informs the internal dance between distraught Neo-Exiles and activated Protectors. Grieving individuals tend to oscillate between being blended (i.e., fully identified with the intense emotions) with the Grief Cluster as it seeks to integrate the meaning of the loss and the Restoration Cluster of inner parts of our personality. The Restoration Cluster of parts within our inner world eventually focus ahead and urge forward action. This mixture of grieving and planning ensures periods of relief during a process that can be intensely painful (Stroebe; Schut, 2010). When the whole internal system has had as much processing time as it needs and all has gone well, the Restoration Cluster will begin to dominate and a new reality that accommodates the loss will be established.

Meanwhile, the meaning of the loss to different parts within our inner world flows through the system slowly, like a wave. Parts can have intense feelings for weeks or months after a loss, as if just realizing what has happened. These are called grief attacks or "being hit with a giant wave," as if at some inner beach. If the person is blindsided by a grief attack or wave, some protective parts may set about distancing and others will do all they can to distract or avoid. The bereaved's Protector parts can be assured that these grief attacks and waves are not a signal that something is wrong; rather they are an opportunity for the bereaved to access their Self-energy within to hold curious and compassionate space to hear and witness grieving parts share what they are experiencing.

What about that which is called Complicated Grief? The Interface of Bereavement and chronic or delayed-onset grief affects roughly fifteen percent of mourners (Kersting, 2004). Complicated Grief is more likely to occur if the individual has experienced significant loss early in life which remains unresolved, traumatic loss or psychiatric illness; especially if the client had a dependent or ambivalent relationship with the deceased (Lobb et al., 2010).

Lack of social support or the mourner's attachment style can complicate grief as well. In 2002, researchers Wayment and Vierthaler discovered that individuals with "an anxious-ambivalent attachment style reported greater levels of grief and depression." (Wayment and Vierthaler, 2011, p. 129). Therapists often see certain strong protective strategies with Complicated Grief that Wolfelt described, including downplaying the importance of a loss by minimizing; converting feelings into physical symptoms by somatising; avoiding grieving by replacing with a new attachment; feeling anger or sadness in relation to other people and events by displacing; and trying to shelve the whole experience by postponing (Wolfelt, 1992). Once a strong protective strategy is identified in therapy, the therapist can ask the protector if the strategy is working and what it believes would happen if it let the client engage with the Loss Cluster.

It helps to not push mourners and to actually have great admiration and respect for Protectors, because grief, when uncomplicated, has its own timetable. In consequence, folkloric wisdom about how long grief ought to last is not helpful and can be hurtful and shaming.

When grief is complex, being curious about which protective parts may be contributing to its chronicity or delayed onset is essential.

Once the Restoration Cluster of parts begin to show up more often in the journey of grief, therapists can attend to and support the natural oscillations between the grief and Restoration clusters. However, when there are no oscillations between grief and Restoration Cluster of parts, it is important to inquire about where the resistance might be occurring. For example, we may notice that a client is mired in the Loss Cluster or, conversely, is only looking ahead (avoiding grief). If the latter, the person is stuck in the agenda of the Restoration Cluster and rarely seeks bereavement counseling or therapy until serious consequences build up. These consequences can be physical ailments, depression, etc.

John Bradshaw once said that "the only way out, is through," as he described his work as an addiction therapist. He also said that emotion can be spelled "e-motion," which to him meant that emotion was "energy in motion." While he was referring to early childhood abuse and trauma that can lead to addition, his metaphor also applies to grief. If we do not process the energy of trauma or grief, then it will find a place to get lodged. It then shows up in the body and it is never good.

Two tragic experiences often result in Complicated Grief: suicide loss, losing a child and unprocessed early traumatic loss (war, murder, accidents, etc.). These losses are terrifyingly random and sudden. The violent death of a child is particularly heart breaking and often evokes a feeling of dread in adults who are parents.

As Wolfelt wrote, "It is out of your helplessness that you ultimately become helpful — 'compassionate curiosity' is what you really need" (Wolfelt, 2006, p. 86).

In grief work our imperative is to acknowledge and welcome a variety of cultural and spiritual beliefs about death. For example, mourners who feel their experience is being pathologized in therapy will avoid sharing information about the continuing relationship they have with the person who has died. A simple question, "Are you still talking to him? Is she showing up for you in some way?" invites this information. In general, normalize and welcome discussion about any and all aspects of a person's grief.

Grieving typically starts with the shock, disbelief and numbness of First Responders. As they give way, the Storyteller often steps in, followed by the Cluster of parts who are actively grieving as well as some parts who blank out and distract to ensure respite from grieving. Finally, our need for balance after profound disruption is so great that we have another set of parts, the Restoration Cluster, whose job is to restore equilibrium. Once they get to work, we oscillate between their efforts to welcome new connections and the grieving we need in order to know the depth of our loss. The job of the therapist and support team is to be a compassionate companion, a witness to the client's experience and sometimes a guide. The role of guide is most relevant when the current circumstance is extreme (as with suicide, homicide and the death of a child) or complicated by unresolved prior loss. Although simple grieving is a matter of keeping company with the client, when grieving is complicated, spend a lot of time validating, reassuring and inviting Protectors to ally with the Self. Keep a particular eye out for physical distress because repressed feelings are often communicated somatically. We all have a history of loss, so we need to notice when we get triggered, ask those parts in us to wait until we are done supporting a mourner and stay in connection with the mourner from our Self-energy, at least from curiosity and compassion.

Therapists and support team members best help their clients, friends and family members who are grieving loss by following the natural oscillations of grieving. This can often means that the mourner shares the same stories or feelings over and over again. It is best to normalize the mourner's investment of energy in the process and to remain alert to early unresolved losses that complicate grieving. In addition, ALL of us who support others who are grieving MUST be aware that our feelings, especially fears, as well as cultural and spiritual beliefs can be obstacles to the mourner's recovery process. Our job throughout is to be vigilant in helping our own triggered inner protective and exiled parts to unblend (move back some to minimize overwhelm), so that we supporters can access our Self-energy, stay present with the mourner's pain and spot Protectors who avoid grieving now because of unsupported loss in the past. Our capacity to both embrace and facilitate Self-led grief "bolsters a life-long practice of learning to trust Self-leadership" (Schwartz, 2013, p. 22) and affords us the opportunity to welcome new connections fully – aware of the possibility that we may lose them and secure in our knowledge that the Self will attend to our grieving parts.

- Derek Scott, RSW

7 CONCLUSION

What do these contributors have in common, and how do they differ? Each was brought up in a milieu where male grief was suppressed. They broke societal taboos to fully acknowledge their grief and to share their stories, although one author chose to remain anonymous. What made them admit their vulnerabilities and to risk their male egos?

The need for catharsis may have provided the strongest impetus, but there was also a desire to help others. Knowing that misery often appreciates good company, sharing is a form of caring. One contributor shared his story (before publication) with several people who were actively grieving, and asked if the work helped them to process their own losses. The feedback was encouraging.

Grief is full of paradox. Not only did the authors collectively survive their dark nights of their souls; all gained something to offset the loss. By admitting their fears and weaknesses they became stronger men; sometimes better partners, neighbors, or friends from the insights and realizations gained from the experience.

Dealing with grief head-on by a willingness to engage in deep reflection and therapy offered the greatest benefits, versus the temptation to self-medicate and temporarily dull the pain.

The inquiry now is, what do we do with all this? It was our desire in writing this book to be role models for what it is like to be a man who perhaps at first, did not do so well with vulnerability, loss and grief. Our culture does not make room for men to feel deeply, to be willing to risk openly expressing our feelings and experiencing loss and grief. As boys, we did feel, we did grieve, we did cry. However, along the way – what appears to be when puberty kicked in, we bought into being "strong," dependable, protective, hunters, providers, focusing ahead on the next mountain to climb and all kinds of missions and projects. While there is nothing wrong with any of that, we sacrificed our emotions and repressed outward expression of the painful emotions.

We found ways to numb out and distract: alcohol, drugs, work, sex, the internet, etc., and we projected our repressed "softness" onto to women, who we treated badly or "others," who we attacked. All men have choices and for many of us, it took entering the second half of life to begin reclaiming our ability to feel and express our feelings.

As Stuart Smith shared in the Introduction to this book:

"Grief is a primal, organic process, if we can allow it to be. Most often, Apollo rules and men seek refuge "upstairs" (why waste time on feelings when there are so many thoughts to entertain?) Intellectualizing feelings is all too familiar to men. The break between head and heart can often render men awkward or speechless. In truth, a man can make himself more complete by embracing the terrifying feelings that come with loss. Loss offers an encounter with meaning, humility, humanity and with love. Stepping into loss can mean stepping into wholeness. There will be inevitable suffering, but there may also be growth. That is a choice."

All four of us risked sharing our journey through the abyss of loss, denial, avoidance and eventual recovery. Our hope in writing this book was to offer the possibility to men, particularly young men, still in the phase of repression, to follow our lead. All of us who contributed to this book are in our 60s. All of us wish we had gotten the lesson of dropping out of our heads and into our hearts in our 20s. However, we did not.

Regardless of what your losses have been, are, or will be, all losses must be grieved. There is no easy way out. In 1988, the late John Bradshaw wrote, Healing the Shame that Binds You. I read the book in 1991, and the one quote of so many wonderful gems in the book that I have never forgotten was:

"There is an old therapeutic adage which states, 'The only way out is through'.".

The only way out is through – not around, not underneath, not over. The pathway through hell is through hell.

Bradshaw was using this quote to address working through toxic shame; however, his quote powerfully addresses the process of grief. There are no short cuts; there are no cures; there are no drugs that will take us through grief, though too many will dull us to the process of grief. Antidepressants have their place, but only if they lift us up enough from despair and total hopelessness so that we can feel the pain of grief and not be stuck in deep depression. If antidepressants are taken, they work best in conjunction with talk therapy with a psychotherapist or grief counselor. Grief is very hard and it is very do-able. One just has to engage it and let their unconscious mind do all the work of processing and slowly moving back and forth between the loss and eventual restoration. We hope this book has offered even just one nugget of supportive gold – if not several. Engage in the journey as life is a short visit between two Great Mysteries.

"There is peace with acceptance and freedom in letting go."
- came to me from within in 1992 during meditation

- Mitch Cohen, M. Ed.

APPENDIX

There Is Much to Grieve – the Many Losses to Grieve
➢ Loss of a pet
➢ Moving to a new location or city
➢ Secondary, anonymous loss (war, tragedy, accidents)
➢ Death of an author, inspirational figure, favorite musician or ideological hero
➢ Loss of health, physical or mental abilities
➢ Loss of an opportunity, a plan, a dream
➢ Rejection, divorce, loss of a relationship, disappearance
➢ Loss of a job, entering retirement
➢ A friend moves away or a work friend leaves the company
➢ Loss of a home, office or other place of significance

What Grief Is
➢ A natural response to loss
➢ A process, rather than a single task: allowing; inviting and participating in thoughts, feelings and expressions of emotion
➢ More organic and emotional than linear and intellectual
➢ Heart-based rather than thinking-based
➢ A wounding, NOT a pathology to be cured or medicated away
➢ Heightened awareness of our own mortality, fear and loss of control
➢ Open-ended: there is no finish line and it is ever-changing
➢ It hurts…. Be with the hurt

Complicated Grief
➢ Suicide
➢ Homicide
➢ Loss of a caregiver (i.e.parent)
➢ Death of a Stillborn, fetal, infant, child
➢ Multiple deaths – simultaneously or sequential in proximity
➢ Death of a twin
➢ Witnessed trauma, violence, war, mutilation
➢ Unresolved loss showing up much later
➢ Death within a clandestine romantic relationship

Source: Stuart Smith, LPC, Survivors of Suicide Support Group Training, June 2, 2023

REFERENCES

10cc, Eric Stewart, Graham Gouldman. "I'm Not in Love." The Original Soundtrack, Mercury, 1975.

Ashworth, D. (2021). You Don't Just Lose Someone Once. https://donnaashworth.com/author/donna/

Becker, E. (2007). *The Denial of Death.* Simon and Schuster.

Bier, S. (Director). (2020). The Undoing [Film]. United States: HBO.

Bradshaw, J. (1988, revised 2005). *Healing the Shame that Binds You.* Health Communications, Inc: Deerfield Beach, FL.

Brener, A. (2001). *Mourning & Mitzvah: A Guided Journal for Walking the Mourner's Path Through Grief to Healing.* Jewish Lights Publishing.

Cohen, L. (1992). Anthem [Song]. On The Future [Album]. Columbia.

Emerson, L., Lake, G., & Palmer, C. (1973). Karn Evil 9 [Song]. On Brain Salad Surgery [Album]. Manticore Records.

Guthrie, W. (1940). This Land Is Your Land [Recorded by Woody Guthrie]. On This Land Is Your Land [Medium of recording]. Folkways Records.

Hallström, L., director. *My Life as a Dog.* Perf. Anton Glanzelius and Tomas von Brömssen, AB Svensk Filmindustri, 1985.

Hunter, R., & Garcia, J. (1970). Ripple [Recorded by Grateful Dead]. On American Beauty [Vinyl]. Warner Bros.

IFS Institute. (n.d.). *IFS Online Circle* [Online program]. https://ifs-institute.com/online-learning

Keller, H. (1929). *We Bereaved.* New York: The Century Co.

Kersting, K. (2004). A New Approach to Complicated Grief. *APA: Monitor on Psychology*, 35(10), 51. http://apa.org/monitor/nov04/grief.aspx

Kubler-Ross, E., Wessler, S., & Avioli, L. V. (1972). On Death and Dying. *JAMA*, *221*(2), 174. https://doi.org/10.1001/jama.1972.03200150040010

Lennon, J., & McCartney, P. (1967). With a Little Help from My Friends [Recorded by The Beatles]. On Sgt. Pepper's Lonely Hearts Club Band [CD]. London: EMI Records.

Lobb, E.A., Kristjanson, L. J., Aoun, S.M., Monterosso, L., Halkett, G.K.B., and Davies, A. (2010). *Predictors of Complicated Grief: A Systematic Review of Empirical Studies. Death Studies*, 34(8), 673-698.

McCartney, P., & McCartney, L. (1971). Ram [Album]. Apple Records.

Michaelson, J. (2009). *Everything is God: The Radical Path of NonDual Judaism*. Trumpeter.

Pink Floyd. (1973). The dark side of the moon [Album]. Harvest Records.

Psychology Today, https://www.psychologytoday.com/us/therapy-types/internal-family-systems-therapy).

Schwartz, R. C. (2013). *The Therapist-Client Relationship and the Transformative Power of Self.*

Scott, Derek (2022). Self-Led Grieving: Transitions, Loss & Death. *IFSCA*.

Scott, Derek "Stepping Stone," an intensive 16-week course. For a complete version of the document from which this chapter was derived, reach out to the *IFSCA* at www.ifsca.ca.

Stein, J., Bock, J., & Harnick, S. (1964). Fiddler on the Roof [Musical]. New York: Imperial Theatre.

Stroebe, M., and Schut, H. (2010). *The Dual Process Model of Coping with Bereavement: A Decade On*. Omega, 61(4), 273-289.

Stroebe, M., Schut, H. (1999) *The Dual Process Model of Coping with Bereavement Rationale and Description, Death Studies*, 23:3, 197-224, DOI: 10.1080/074811899201046.

Sweezy, M. and Ziskind, E. (Editors), *IFS Innovations and Elaborations in Internal Family Systems Therapy. Chapter 5: "Self-led Grieving: Transitions, Loss and*

Death," by Derek Scott. (Routledge of Taylor and Francis Group: New York), 2017, pp 90-108.

Sweezy, M. and Ziskind, E.L. (Editors.), *Internal Family Systems Therapy: New Dimensions (1-23).* New York: Routledge.

The Beatles. "Here Comes the Sun." Abbey Road, Apple Records, 1969.

Towner, R. (1987). "Beneath An Evening Sky" originally appeared on a 1979 release "Old Friends, New Friends," but later appeared on Slide Show (with Gary Burton), Oregon's 45th Parallel and Oregon in Moscow. Beneath an Evening Sky [Recorded by Ralph Towner]. On City of Eyes [CD]. Munich: ECM.

Wayment, H.A., & Vierthaler, J. (2011). Attachment Style and Bereavement Reactions. *Journal of Loss and Trauma: International Perspectives on Stress and Coping,* 7(2), 129-149. Retrieved from http://dx.doi.org/10.1080/153250202753472291.

Weller, F. (2015). *The Wild Edge of Sorrow: Rituals of Renewal and the Sacred Work of Grief.* North Atlantic Books.

Whitfield, N. & Strong, B. (1972). Papa Was a Rollin' Stone [Recorded by The Temptations]. On All Directions [Vinyl]. Gordy.

Wolfelt, A. D. (1992). *Understanding Grief: Helping Yourself Heal.* Bristol, PA: Accelerated Development.

Wolfelt, A. D. (2006). *Companioning the Bereaved.* Fort Collins, CO: Companion Press.

WHO ARE YOU?

Mitch Cohen, M. Ed.

Mitch is an Internal Family Systems (IFS) and Enneagram Coach Practitioner, Spiritual Director and Grief Counselor. He was Certified as a Life Coach in 2002, and his focus is on suicide-related grief, loss and difficult life transitions. Mitch facilitates a Survivors of Suicide support peer group, providing a space for everyone in the room to share their Complicated Grief journey.

Mitch has completed extensive training and practice in IFS with both the IFS Institute and IFS Counseling Association and is an International Enneagram Association Accredited Professional. A former Rabbi, Mitch graduated in May 2020 from the Zeitgeist Atlanta Non-faith-based Spiritual Director program. He supports anyone on their individual personal spiritual journey, regardless of their beliefs or past observance or faith tradition - or no faith tradition. An area of focus is recovery from religious trauma.

Among the causes he supports are: The Link Counseling Center, The IFS Foundation, One River Foundation and Zeitgeist Atlanta: The Interfaith Home for the Spiritually Independent. Mitch serves on the Board of Zeitgeist Atlanta.

Jon Yaeger

Jon Yaeger and his family live in Atlanta, GA. Jon graduated from Emory University with a B.A. in English and also attended Georgia State University's Masters of Public Health graduate studies program.

He is a small business entrepreneur and a member of Rotary and Lions club service organizations. Jon is currently working with major volunteer organizations to collaborate on global health initiatives.

His hobby is sound-systems electronics, and Jon spends many hours repairing older stereo receivers into updated, tube-amp receivers, which are in high demand by his friends.

Stuart Smith, LPC

Stuart Smith is a psychotherapist with a private practice in Atlanta and is a staff clinician at the Link Counseling Center. He served as the Clinical Coordinator for The Link's Resource Center for Suicide Prevention and Aftercare for six years. He has a Master's Degree in Interdisciplinary Humanities with an emphasis in Depth Psychology as well as a Master's in Human Development and Psychological Counseling. He also holds post-graduate certificates in Addictions Counseling and Expressive Arts Therapy. While he is heavily involved in grief therapy, he serves many individuals, couples, and families for a broad range of therapeutic concerns.

In addition to his work as a psychotherapist he has worked in education and in the arts in support of his interest in creativity and the promotion of life-long learning. He has lectured and taught college classes on a range of topics including counseling theory, the arts, human relations, and cultural history. He maintains interests in humanistic and Depth Psychology, mindfulness and nature studies. Stuart offers presentations and workshops on a number of subjects and is on the advisory board of the C.G. Jung Society of Atlanta.

Derek Scott, RSW

Derek Scott, RSW is a registered social worker and Certified IFS (Internal Family Systems) therapist and consultant. He is the founder of IFSCA– an organization dedicated to bringing awareness of the IFS model to counselors and therapists in Canada and beyond. Through IFSCA he offers online courses teaching the IFS model.

Derek has worked in the field of counseling/therapy for over 35 years, including 15 working exclusively as an IFS therapist and 18 years as an AIDS counselor specializing in multiple loss. He is a popular guest lecturer in the department of Thanatology at the University of Western Ontario and has presented at numerous national and international conferences.

Lori Conway

Lori Conway began her professional career as a technical editor, where she met Mitch Cohen and, in his words, taught him to write. She then gravitated through a variety of jobs, from lab technician to golf course manager to professional gardener to mother to environmental consultant to native plant habitat manager. She hopes to spend her remaining years inspiring a more conservation-minded land use that incorporates native plants and sustainable landscape practices in urban green spaces, believing that we all need time and places to commune with nature no matter where we live.

Lori considers herself a jack of some trades, master of none, but likes to think she was gifted with an ability to listen, tease out the underlying truth of a situation, and follow that truth to help resolve conflict and foster progress. She is fascinated with the reasons why people behave as they do, believing that we all are a product of our life experiences, both good and bad. She is in awe of people who wrestle with heartbreaking tragedies and manage to keep going while riding the ebb and flow of emotions that accompany profound loss.

Lori has borne witness to the effects of avoiding grief, how it stunts emotional development and impedes fulfillment of one's potential. She believes people who work through grief in a healthy way can develop a sanguine resilience that those of us who are "fortunate" to avoid profound loss in life could envy.

She is honored and grateful for the opportunity to contribute to this worthwhile project. She hopes it helps other men to embrace the anguishing work of grieving and inspires their friends and family to provide compassionate support as these men navigate their troubled waters toward peace and fortitude to move forward with living life.

Suzanne Bonnard Quillian

Suzanne is recently and permanently retired from a 35-year career in technical writing. She started writing out her unexpressed emotions around the age of 10. The written word became her only means of surviving the turmoil and trouble of a damaged and struggling family. The written page was her solace and her guide.

In 1984, in Athens, GA, she found writing could be a force of love and not just a way to release and survive pain and loss. She wrote articles for Tasty World Magazine, reviewing and interviewing bands and musicians from places far and wide. After graduating from the University of Georgia in 1987, her writing evolved again in order to provide a living. She started a series of editing/writing jobs, and in 1989 was happily dragged into the environmental field by Lori Conway, who also happily dragged her into this book.

Working on the Men and Grief project brought her full circle, back to understanding how writing (and reading) is a way of talking yourself through it all.

"As I started reading the stories, the tears just started flowing. It took me a long time to read this book, switching back from the emotional to do the non-emotional work of editing. Ultimately, it's the work of grief that we all must do to recover. As I stood in each man's story, feeling it with sympathy and empathy, I reimagined my own story, as if I were telling it to them. Dear Reader, you don't have to share your story in a book or even with another human being, but you must share it with yourself. Sit down with each of these men and talk about it. Perhaps you will find, as I did, that restoration, healing, and yes, even happiness, come quietly sometimes, when you aren't even expecting them anymore. This book is a gift, open it."

Candice Dyer

Candice Dyer is a writer and editor based in north Georgia. She was a staff writer for Atlanta magazine, and her work has appeared in publications such as Garden & Gun, Men's Journal, Country Living, The Atlanta Journal-Constitution, and other publications. She is the author of Street Singers, Soul Shakers, Rebels with a Cause: Music from Macon.

Steven J. Gold

Steve is a long-time lover of Silence and meditation practitioner and teacher. He has authored several books on spirituality from a Torah-Veda perspective, a children's book, and is an editor and contributor to a book of poems, *Breaking the Silence; Poems of Spiritual Luminescence.* Steve helped with a final polishing up of formatting, in addition to other guidance on technical matters. Om Shalom.

Made in the USA
Columbia, SC
15 August 2023

21588852R00072